Connected Mathematics 2™

Accentuate the Negative

Integers and Rational Numbers

Glenda Lappan
James T. Fey
William M. Fitzgerald
Susan N. Friel
Elizabeth Difanis Phillips

PEARSON

Prentice Hall

Boston, Massachusetts
Upper Saddle River, New Jersey

Connected Mathematics™ was developed at Michigan State University with financial support from the Michigan State University Office of the Provost, Computing and Technology, and the College of Natural Science.

This material is based upon work supported by the National Science Foundation under Grant No. MDR 9150217 and Grant No. ESI 9986372. Opinions expressed are those of the authors and not necessarily those of the Foundation.

The Michigan State University authors and administration have agreed that all MSU royalties arising from this publication will be devoted to purposes supported by the MSU Mathematics Education Enrichment Fund.

ISBN 0-13-165641-4

7 8 9 10   09 08

Authors of Connected Mathematics

(from left to right) Glenda Lappan, Betty Phillips, Susan Friel, Bill Fitzgerald, Jim Fey

Glenda Lappan is a University Distinguished Professor in the Department of Mathematics at Michigan State University. Her research and development interests are in the connected areas of students' learning of mathematics and mathematics teachers' professional growth and change related to the development and enactment of K–12 curriculum materials.

James T. Fey is a Professor of Curriculum and Instruction and Mathematics at the University of Maryland. His consistent professional interest has been development and research focused on curriculum materials that engage middle and high school students in problem-based collaborative investigations of mathematical ideas and their applications.

William M. Fitzgerald *(Deceased)* was a Professor in the Department of Mathematics at Michigan State University. His early research was on the use of concrete materials in supporting student learning and led to the development of teaching materials for laboratory environments. Later he helped develop a teaching model to support student experimentation with mathematics.

Susan N. Friel is a Professor of Mathematics Education in the School of Education at the University of North Carolina at Chapel Hill. Her research interests focus on statistics education for middle-grade students and, more broadly, on teachers' professional development and growth in teaching mathematics K–8.

Elizabeth Difanis Phillips is a Senior Academic Specialist in the Mathematics Department of Michigan State University. She is interested in teaching and learning mathematics for both teachers and students. These interests have led to curriculum and professional development projects at the middle school and high school levels, as well as projects related to the teaching and learning of algebra across the grades.

CMP2 Development Staff

Teacher Collaborator in Residence
Yvonne Grant
Michigan State University

Administrative Assistant
Judith Martus Miller
Michigan State University

Production and Field Site Manager
Lisa Keller
Michigan State University

Technical and Editorial Support
Brin Keller, Peter Lappan, Jim Laser,
Michael Masterson, Stacey Miceli

Assessment Team
June Bailey and Debra Sobko (Apollo Middle School, Rochester, New York), George Bright (University of North Carolina, Greensboro), Gwen Ranzau Campbell (Sunrise Park Middle School, White Bear Lake, Minnesota), Holly DeRosia, Kathy Dole, and Teri Keusch (Portland Middle School, Portland, Michigan), Mary Beth Schmitt (Traverse City East Junior High School, Traverse City, Michigan), Genni Steele (Central Middle School, White Bear Lake, Minnesota), Jacqueline Stewart (Okemos, Michigan), Elizabeth Tye (Magnolia Junior High School, Magnolia, Arkansas)

Development Assistants
At Lansing Community College *Undergraduate Assistant:* James Brinegar

At Michigan State University *Graduate Assistants:* Dawn Berk, Emily Bouck, Bulent Buyukbozkirli, Kuo-Liang Chang, Christopher Danielson, Srinivasa Dharmavaram, Deb Johanning, Wesley Kretzschmar, Kelly Rivette, Sarah Sword, Tat Ming Sze, Marie Turini, Jeffrey Wanko; *Undergraduate Assistants:* Daniel Briggs, Jeffrey Chapin, Jade Corsé, Elisha Hardy, Alisha Harold, Elizabeth Keusch, Julia Letoutchaia, Karen Loeffler, Brian Oliver, Carl Oliver, Evonne Pedawi, Lauren Rebrovich

At the University of Maryland *Graduate Assistants:* Kim Harris Bethea, Kara Karch

At the University of North Carolina (Chapel Hill) *Graduate Assistants:* Mark Ellis, Trista Stearns; *Undergraduate Assistant:* Daniel Smith

Advisory Board for CMP2

Thomas Banchoff
Professor of Mathematics
Brown University
Providence, Rhode Island

Anne Bartel
Mathematics Coordinator
Minneapolis Public Schools
Minneapolis, Minnesota

Hyman Bass
Professor of Mathematics
University of Michigan
Ann Arbor, Michigan

Joan Ferrini-Mundy
Associate Dean of the College of
Natural Science; Professor
Michigan State University
East Lansing, Michigan

James Hiebert
Professor
University of Delaware
Newark, Delaware

Susan Hudson Hull
Charles A. Dana Center
University of Texas
Austin, Texas

Michele Luke
Mathematics Curriculum
Coordinator
West Junior High
Minnetonka, Minnesota

Kay McClain
Assistant Professor of
Mathematics Education
Vanderbilt University
Nashville, Tennessee

Edward Silver
Professor; Chair of Educational
Studies
University of Michigan
Ann Arbor, Michigan

Judith Sowder
Professor Emerita
San Diego State University
San Diego, California

Lisa Usher
Mathematics Resource Teacher
California Academy of
Mathematics and Science
San Pedro, California

Field Test Sites for CMP2

During the development of the revised edition of *Connected Mathematics* (CMP2), more than 100 classroom teachers have field-tested materials at 49 school sites in 12 states and the District of Columbia. This classroom testing occurred over three academic years (2001 through 2004), allowing careful study of the effectiveness of each of the 24 units that comprise the program. A special thanks to the students and teachers at these pilot schools.

Arkansas
Magnolia Public Schools
Kittena Bell*, Judith Trowell*; *Central Elementary School:* Maxine Broom, Betty Eddy, Tiffany Fallin, Bonnie Flurry, Carolyn Monk, Elizabeth Tye; *Magnolia Junior High School:* Monique Bryan, Ginger Cook, David Graham, Shelby Lamkin

Colorado
Boulder Public Schools
Nevin Platt Middle School: Judith Koenig

St. Vrain Valley School District, Longmont
Westview Middle School: Colleen Beyer, Kitty Canupp, Ellie Decker*, Peggy McCarthy, Tanya deNobrega, Cindy Payne, Ericka Pilon, Andrew Roberts

District of Columbia
Capitol Hill Day School: Ann Lawrence

Georgia
University of Georgia, Athens
Brad Findell

Madison Public Schools
Morgan County Middle School: Renee Burgdorf, Lynn Harris, Nancy Kurtz, Carolyn Stewart

Maine
Falmouth Public Schools
Falmouth Middle School: Donna Erikson, Joyce Hebert, Paula Hodgkins, Rick Hogan, David Legere, Cynthia Martin, Barbara Stiles, Shawn Towle*

* indicates a Field Test Site Coordinator

Michigan
Portland Public Schools
Portland Middle School: Mark Braun, Holly DeRosia, Kathy Dole*, Angie Foote, Teri Keusch, Tammi Wardwell

Traverse City Area Public Schools
Bertha Vos Elementary: Kristin Sak; *Central Grade School:* Michelle Clark; Jody Meyers; *Eastern Elementary:* Karrie Tufts; *Interlochen Elementary:* Mary McGee-Cullen; *Long Lake Elementary:* Julie Faulkner*, Charlie Maxbauer, Katherine Sleder; *Norris Elementary:* Hope Slanaker; *Oak Park Elementary:* Jessica Steed; *Traverse Heights Elementary:* Jennifer Wolfert; *Westwoods Elementary:* Nancy Conn; *Old Mission Peninsula School:* Deb Larimer; *Traverse City East Junior High:* Ivanka Berkshire, Ruthanne Kladder, Jan Palkowski, Jane Peterson, Mary Beth Schmitt; *Traverse City West Junior High:* Dan Fouch*, Ray Fouch

Sturgis Public Schools
Sturgis Middle School: Ellen Eisele

Minnesota
Burnsville School District 191
Hidden Valley Elementary: Stephanie Cin, Jane McDevitt

Hopkins School District 270
Alice Smith Elementary: Sandra Cowing, Kathleen Gustafson, Martha Mason, Scott Stillman; *Eisenhower Elementary:* Chad Bellig, Patrick Berger, Nancy Glades, Kye Johnson, Shane Wasserman, Victoria Wilson; *Gatewood Elementary:* Sarah Ham, Julie Kloos, Janine Pung, Larry Wade; *Glen Lake Elementary:* Jacqueline Cramer, Kathy Hering, Cecelia Morris,

Robb Trenda; *Katherine Curren Elementary:* Diane Bancroft, Sue DeWit, John Wilson; *L. H. Tanglen Elementary:* Kevin Athmann, Lisa Becker, Mary LaBelle, Kathy Rezac, Roberta Severson; *Meadowbrook Elementary:* Jan Gauger, Hildy Shank, Jessica Zimmerman; *North Junior High:* Laurel Hahn, Kristin Lee, Jodi Markuson, Bruce Mestemacher, Laurel Miller, Bonnie Rinker, Jeannine Salzer, Sarah Shafer, Cam Stottler; *West Junior High:* Alicia Beebe, Kristie Earl, Nobu Fujii, Pam Georgetti, Susan Gilbert, Regina Nelson Johnson, Debra Lindstrom, Michele Luke*, Jon Sorenson

Minneapolis School District 1
Ann Sullivan K-8 School: Bronwyn Collins; Anne Bartel* (Curriculum and Instruction Office)

Wayzata School District 284
Central Middle School: Sarajane Myers, Dan Nielsen, Tanya Ravnholdt

White Bear Lake School District 624
Central Middle School: Amy Jorgenson, Michelle Reich, Brenda Sammon

New York
New York City Public Schools
IS 89: Yelena Aynbinder, Chi-Man Ng, Nina Rapaport, Joel Spengler, Phyllis Tam*, Brent Wyso; *Wagner Middle School:* Jason Appel, Intissar Fernandez, Yee Gee Get, Richard Goldstein, Irving Marcus, Sue Norton, Bernadita Owens, Jennifer Rehn*, Kevin Yuhas

Ohio
Talawanda School District, Oxford
Talawanda Middle School: Teresa Abrams, Larry Brock, Heather Brosey, Julie Churchman, Monna Even, Karen Fitch, Bob George, Amanda Klee, Pat Meade, Sandy Montgomery, Barbara Sherman, Lauren Steidl

Miami University
Jeffrey Wanko*

Springfield Public Schools
Rockway School: Jim Mamer

Pennsylvania
Pittsburgh Public Schools
Kenneth Labuskes, Marianne O'Connor, Mary Lynn Raith*; *Arthur J. Rooney Middle School:* David Hairston, Stamatina Mousetis, Alfredo Zangaro; *Frick International Studies Academy:* Suzanne Berry, Janet Falkowski, Constance Finseth, Romika Hodge, Frank Machi; *Reizenstein Middle School:* Jeff Baldwin, James Brautigam, Lorena Burnett, Glen Cobbett, Michael Jordan, Margaret Lazur, Melissa Munnell, Holly Neely, Ingrid Reed, Dennis Reft

Texas
Austin Independent School District
Bedichek Middle School: Lisa Brown, Jennifer Glasscock, Vicki Massey

El Paso Independent School District
Cordova Middle School: Armando Aguirre, Anneliesa Durkes, Sylvia Guzman, Pat Holguin*, William Holguin, Nancy Nava, Laura Orozco, Michelle Peña, Roberta Rosen, Patsy Smith, Jeremy Wolf

Plano Independent School District
Patt Henry, James Wohlgehagen*; *Frankford Middle School:* Mandy Baker, Cheryl Butsch, Amy Dudley, Betsy Eshelman, Janet Greene, Cort Haynes, Kathy Letchworth, Kay Marshall, Kelly McCants, Amy Reck, Judy Scott, Syndy Snyder, Lisa Wang; *Wilson Middle School:* Darcie Bane, Amanda Bedenko, Whitney Evans, Tonelli Hatley, Sarah (Becky) Higgs, Kelly Johnston, Rebecca McElligott, Kay Neuse, Cheri Slocum, Kelli Straight

Washington
Evergreen School District
Shahala Middle School: Nicole Abrahamsen, Terry Coon*, Carey Doyle, Sheryl Drechsler, George Gemma, Gina Helland, Amy Hilario, Darla Lidyard, Sean McCarthy, Tilly Meyer, Willow Neuwelt, Todd Parsons, Brian Pederson, Stan Posey, Shawn Scott, Craig Sjoberg, Lynette Sundstrom, Charles Switzer, Luke Youngblood

Wisconsin
Beaver Dam Unified School District
Beaver Dam Middle School: Jim Braemer, Jeanne Frick, Jessica Greatens, Barbara Link, Dennis McCormick, Karen Michels, Nancy Nichols*, Nancy Palm, Shelly Stelsel, Susan Wiggins

---

* indicates a Field Test Site Coordinator

Reviews of CMP to Guide Development of CMP2

Before writing for CMP2 began or field tests were conducted, the first edition of *Connected Mathematics* was submitted to the mathematics faculties of school districts from many parts of the country and to 80 individual reviewers for extensive comments.

School District Survey Reviews of CMP

Arizona
Madison School District #38 (Phoenix)

Arkansas
Cabot School District, Little Rock School District, Magnolia School District

California
Los Angeles Unified School District

Colorado
St. Vrain Valley School District (Longmont)

Florida
Leon County Schools (Tallahassee)

Illinois
School District #21 (Wheeling)

Indiana
Joseph L. Block Junior High (East Chicago)

Kentucky
Fayette County Public Schools (Lexington)

Maine
Selection of Schools

Massachusetts
Selection of Schools

Michigan
Sparta Area Schools

Minnesota
Hopkins School District

Texas
Austin Independent School District, The El Paso Collaborative for Academic Excellence, Plano Independent School District

Wisconsin
Platteville Middle School

Individual Reviewers of CMP

Arkansas
Deborah Cramer; Robby Frizzell *(Taylor)*; Lowell Lynde *(University of Arkansas, Monticello)*; Leigh Manzer *(Norfork)*; Lynne Roberts *(Emerson High School, Emerson)*; Tony Timms *(Cabot Public Schools)*; Judith Trowell *(Arkansas Department of Higher Education)*

California
José Alcantar *(Gilroy)*; Eugenie Belcher *(Gilroy)*; Marian Pasternack *(Lowman M. S. T. Center, North Hollywood)*; Susana Pezoa *(San Jose)*; Todd Rabusin *(Hollister)*; Margaret Siegfried *(Ocala Middle School, San Jose)*; Polly Underwood *(Ocala Middle School, San Jose)*

Colorado
Janeane Golliher *(St. Vrain Valley School District, Longmont)*; Judith Koenig *(Nevin Platt Middle School, Boulder)*

Florida
Paige Loggins *(Swift Creek Middle School, Tallahassee)*

Illinois
Jan Robinson *(School District #21, Wheeling)*

Indiana
Frances Jackson *(Joseph L. Block Junior High, East Chicago)*

Kentucky
Natalee Feese *(Fayette County Public Schools, Lexington)*

Maine
Betsy Berry *(Maine Math & Science Alliance, Augusta)*

Maryland
Joseph Gagnon *(University of Maryland, College Park)*; Paula Maccini *(University of Maryland, College Park)*

Massachusetts
George Cobb *(Mt. Holyoke College, South Hadley)*; Cliff Kanold *(University of Massachusetts, Amherst)*

Michigan
Mary Bouck *(Farwell Area Schools)*; Carol Dorer *(Slauson Middle School, Ann Arbor)*; Carrie Heaney *(Forsythe Middle School, Ann Arbor)*; Ellen Hopkins *(Clague Middle School, Ann Arbor)*; Teri Keusch *(Portland Middle School, Portland)*; Valerie Mills *(Oakland Schools, Waterford)*; Mary Beth Schmitt *(Traverse City East Junior High, Traverse City)*; Jack Smith *(Michigan State University, East Lansing)*; Rebecca Spencer *(Sparta Middle School, Sparta)*; Ann Marie Nicoll Turner *(Tappan Middle School, Ann Arbor)*; Scott Turner *(Scarlett Middle School, Ann Arbor)*

Minnesota
Margarita Alvarez *(Olson Middle School, Minneapolis)*; Jane Amundson *(Nicollet Junior High, Burnsville)*; Anne Bartel *(Minneapolis Public Schools)*; Gwen Ranzau Campbell *(Sunrise Park Middle School, White Bear Lake)*; Stephanie Cin *(Hidden Valley Elementary, Burnsville)*; Joan Garfield *(University of Minnesota, Minneapolis)*; Gretchen Hall *(Richfield Middle School, Richfield)*; Jennifer Larson *(Olson Middle School, Minneapolis)*; Michele Luke *(West Junior High, Minnetonka)*; Jeni Meyer *(Richfield Junior High, Richfield)*; Judy Pfingsten *(Inver Grove Heights Middle School, Inver Grove Heights)*; Sarah Shafer *(North Junior High, Minnetonka)*; Genni Steele *(Central Middle School, White Bear Lake)*; Victoria Wilson *(Eisenhower Elementary, Hopkins)*; Paul Zorn *(St. Olaf College, Northfield)*

New York
Debra Altenau-Bartolino *(Greenwich Village Middle School, New York)*; Doug Clements *(University of Buffalo)*; Francis Curcio *(New York University, New York)*; Christine Dorosh *(Clinton School for Writers, Brooklyn)*; Jennifer Rehn *(East Side Middle School, New York)*; Phyllis Tam *(IS 89 Lab School, New York)*; Marie Turini *(Louis Armstrong Middle School, New York)*; Lucy West *(Community School District 2, New York)*; Monica Witt *(Simon Baruch Intermediate School 104, New York)*

Pennsylvania
Robert Aglietti *(Pittsburgh)*; Sharon Mihalich *(Pittsburgh)*; Jennifer Plumb *(South Hills Middle School, Pittsburgh)*; Mary Lynn Raith *(Pittsburgh Public Schools)*

Texas
Michelle Bittick *(Austin Independent School District)*; Margaret Cregg *(Plano Independent School District)*; Sheila Cunningham *(Klein Independent School District)*; Judy Hill *(Austin Independent School District)*; Patricia Holguin *(El Paso Independent School District)*; Bonnie McNemar *(Arlington)*; Kay Neuse *(Plano Independent School District)*; Joyce Polanco *(Austin Independent School District)*; Marge Ramirez *(University of Texas at El Paso)*; Pat Rossman *(Baker Campus, Austin)*; Cindy Schimek *(Houston)*; Cynthia Schneider *(Charles A. Dana Center, University of Texas at Austin)*; Uri Treisman *(Charles A. Dana Center, University of Texas at Austin)*; Jacqueline Weilmuenster *(Grapevine-Colleyville Independent School District)*; LuAnn Weynand *(San Antonio)*; Carmen Whitman *(Austin Independent School District)*; James Wohlgehagen *(Plano Independent School District)*

Washington
Ramesh Gangolli *(University of Washington, Seattle)*

Wisconsin
Susan Lamon *(Marquette University, Hales Corner)*; Steve Reinhart *(retired, Chippewa Falls Middle School, Eau Claire)*

Table of Contents

Accentuate the Negative
Integers and Rational Numbers

Unit Opener 2

Mathematical Highlights 4

Investigation 1 Extending the Number System 5

1.1 Playing Math Fever: Using Positive and Negative Numbers 8

1.2 From Sauna to Snowbank: Comparing and Ordering
Positive and Negative Numbers 10

1.3 What's the Change?: Using a Number Line Model 12

1.4 In the Chips: Using a Chip Model 14

ACE Homework 16

Mathematical Reflections 21

Investigation 2 Adding and Subtracting Integers 22

2.1 Introducing Addition of Integers 22

2.2 Introducing Subtraction of Integers 24

2.3 The "+/−" Connection: Addition and Subtraction
Relationships 28

2.4 Fact Families 30

2.5 Coordinate Graphing 30

ACE Homework 32

Mathematical Reflections 41

Investigation 3 **Multiplying and Dividing Integers** **42**

3.1 Introducing Multiplication of Integers **44**

3.2 Multiplication Patterns **46**

3.3 Introducing Division of Integers **47**

3.4 Playing the Integer Product Game: Multiplying Integers **48**

ACE Homework **50**

Mathematical Reflections **59**

Investigation 4 **Properties of Operations** **60**

4.1 Order of Operations **60**

4.2 Distributing Operations **64**

4.3 The Distributive Property and Subtraction **66**

ACE Homework **69**

Mathematical Reflections **75**

Unit Project: Dealing Down **76**

Looking Back and Looking Ahead **78**

English/Spanish Glossary **80**

Index **83**

Acknowledgments **85**

Accentuate the Negative

Integers and Rational Numbers

After the first five questions in a quiz show, player A has a score of −100 and player B has a score of −150. Which player has the lead and how great is the lead?

Hahn competes in a relay race. He goes from the 0 meter line to the 15 meter line in 5 seconds. At what rate (distance per second) does he run?

A new convenience store wants to attract customers. For a one-day special, they sell gasoline for $0.25 below their cost. They sell 5,750 gallons that day. How much money do they lose?

Most of the numbers you have worked with in math class this year have been greater than or equal to zero. However, numbers less than zero can provide important information. Winter temperatures in many places fall below 0°F. Businesses that lose money have profits less than $0. Scores in games or sports can be less than zero.

Numbers greater than zero are called *positive numbers*. Numbers less than zero are called *negative numbers*. In *Accentuate the Negative,* you will work with both positive and negative numbers. One subset of positive and negative numbers that you will study is called *integers*. You will explore models that help you think about adding, subtracting, multiplying, and dividing positive and negative numbers. You will also learn more about the properties of operations on positive and negative numbers.

In *Accentuate the Negative,* you will solve problems similar to those on the previous page that require understanding and skill in working with positive and negative numbers.

Mathematical Highlights

Integers and Rational Numbers

In *Accentuate the Negative*, you will extend your knowledge of negative numbers. You will explore ways to use negative numbers in solving problems.

You will learn how to

- Use appropriate notation to indicate positive and negative numbers
- Compare and order positive and negative rational numbers (fractions, decimals, and zero) and locate them on a number line
- Understand the relationship between a positive or negative number and its opposite (additive inverse)
- Develop algorithms for adding, subtracting, multiplying, and dividing positive and negative numbers
- Write mathematical sentences to show relationships
- Write and use related fact families for addition/subtraction and multiplication/division to solve simple equations
- Use parentheses and rules for the order of operations in computations
- Understand and use the Commutative Property for addition and multiplication
- Apply the Distributive Property to simplify expressions and solve problems
- Graph points in four quadrants
- Use positive and negative numbers to model and answer questions about problem situations

As you work on problems in this unit, ask yourself questions like these:

How do negative and positive numbers help in describing the situation?

What will addition, subtraction, multiplication, or division of positive and negative numbers tell about the problem?

What model(s) for positive and negative numbers would help in showing the relationships in the problem situation?

Investigation 1

Extending the Number System

In your study of numbers, you have focused on operations (+, −, ×, and ÷) with whole numbers, fractions, and decimals. In this unit, you will learn about some important new numbers in the number system.

Suppose you start with a number line showing 0, 1, 2, 3, 4, and 5.

Take the number line and fold it around the zero point. Make marks on the left side of zero to match the marks on the right side.

Label the new marks with numbers that have negative signs (⁻). These numbers (to the left of 0) are **negative numbers.**

I owe my Dad 3 dollars, so I have ⁻3 dollars.

Each negative number is paired with a **positive number.** The numbers in the pair are the same distance from zero but in opposite directions on the number line. These number pairs are called **opposites.** You can label positive numbers with positive signs (⁺).

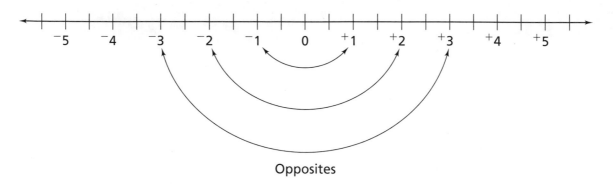

Opposites

Some subsets of the positive and negative numbers have special names. Whole numbers and their opposites are called **integers** (⁻4, ⁻3, ⁻2, ⁻1, 0, ⁺1, ⁺2, ⁺3, ⁺4).

Fractions also have opposites. For example, $^+\frac{1}{2}$ and $^-\frac{1}{2}$ are opposites. Positive and negative integers and fractions are called rational numbers. **Rational numbers** are numbers that can be expressed as one integer divided by another integer.

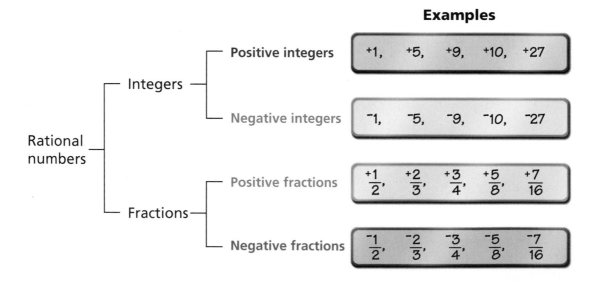

In mathematical notation, you can write a positive number with a raised plus sign ($^+$150) or without any sign (150). You can write a negative number with a raised minus sign ($^-$150). To avoid confusion with operation signs, it is common to use raised signs.

Many calculators have a special negative number key . When you press 5 ▬ (-) 2 , the calculator shows "5 − $^-$2."

Getting Ready for Problem 1.1

- Where would the following pairs of numbers be located on the number line?

  $^+$7 and $^-$7

  $^+$2.7 and $^-$2.7

  $^-$3.8 and $^+$3.8

  $-\frac{1}{2}$ and $^+\frac{1}{2}$

  $4\frac{3}{4}$ and $^-4\frac{3}{4}$

- If the same relationship holds true for all numbers, what would be the opposite of $^-1\frac{2}{3}$ and where would it be located?

Ms. Bernoski's math classes often play Math Fever, a game similar to a popular television game show. The game board is shown. Below each category name are five cards. The front of each card shows a point value. The back of each card has a question related to the category. Cards with higher point values have more difficult questions.

Math Fever

Operations With Fractions	Similarity	Probability	Area and Perimeter	Tiling the Plane	Factors and Multiples
50	50	50	50	50	50
100	100	100	100	100	100
150	150	150	150	150	150
200	200	200	200	200	200
250	250	250	250	250	250

The game is played in teams. One team starts the game by choosing a card. The teacher asks the question on the back of the card. The first team to answer the question correctly gets the point value on the card. The card is then removed from the board. If a team answers the question incorrectly, the point value is subtracted from their score. The team that answers correctly chooses the next category and point value.

At one point in a game, the scores are as follows:

Super Brains	Rocket Scientists	Know-It-Alls
⁻300	150	⁻500

A. Which team has the highest score? Which team has the lowest score? Explain.

B. What is the difference in points for each pair of teams?

C. Use number sentences to describe two possible ways that each team reached its score.

D. The current scores are ⁻300 for Super Brains, 150 for Rocket Scientists, and ⁻500 for Know-It-Alls.

    1. Write number sentences to represent each sequence of points. Start with the current score for each team.

      a. Super Brains

Point Value	Answer
200	Correct
150	Incorrect
50	Correct
50	Correct

      b. Rocket Scientists

Point Value	Answer
50	Incorrect
200	Incorrect
100	Correct
150	Incorrect

      c. Know-It-Alls

Point Value	Answer
100	Incorrect
200	Correct
150	Incorrect
50	Incorrect

    2. Now which team has the highest score? Which team has the lowest score?

    3. What is the difference in points for each pair of teams?

E. The number sentences below describe what happens at a particular point during a game of Math Fever. Find each missing number. Explain what each sentence tells about a team's performance and overall score.

    1. BrainyActs: ⁻200 + 150 − 100 = ▪

    2. MathSperts: 450 − 200 = ▪

    3. ExCells: 200 − 250 = ▪

    4. SuperMs: ⁻350 + ▪ = ⁻150

ACE   **Homework starts on page 16.**

The record high and low temperatures in the United States are 134°F in Death Valley, California and ⁻80°F in Prospect Creek, Alaska. Imagine going from 134°F to ⁻80°F in an instant!

In Finland, people think that such temperature shocks are fun and good for your health. This activity is called sauna-bathing.

In the winter, Finnish people sit for a certain amount of time in sauna houses. The houses are heated as high as 120°F. Then the people run outside, where the temperature might be as low as ⁻20°F.

Inside the Sauna   **Outside in Snow**

The two thermometers shown are similar to number lines. One horizontal number line can show the same information as the two thermometers.

On the number line, a move to the left is a move in a negative direction. The numbers decrease in value. A move to the right is a move in a positive direction. The numbers increase in value. On the thermometers, a move down means the number values decrease and the temperatures get colder. A move up means the number values increase and the temperatures get hotter.

Problem 1.2 Comparing and Ordering Positive and Negative Numbers

Sketch number lines to show your reasoning.

A. Order these temperatures from least to greatest.

0°F   115°F   ⁻15°F   ⁻32.5°F   ⁻40°F   113.2°F   ⁻32.7°F

B. For each pair of temperatures, identify which temperature is further from ⁻2°F.

1. 6°F or ⁻6°F?   **2.** ⁻7°F or 3°F?

3. 2°F or ⁻5°F?   **4.** ⁻10°F or 7°F?

C. Identify the temperature that is halfway between each pair of temperatures.

1. 0°F and 10°F   **2.** ⁻5°F and 15°F

3. 5°F and ⁻15°F   **4.** 0°F and ⁻20°F

5. ⁻8°F and 8°F   **6.** ⁻6°F and 6°F

7. During one week, the high temperature was 60°F. The halfway temperature was 15°F. What was the low temperature?

D. Name six temperatures between ⁻2°F and ⁺1°F. Order them from least to greatest.

E. 1. Estimate values for points A–E.

2. How does the number line help you find the smaller value of two numbers?

F. What are the opposites of these numbers?

1. 3   **2.** 7.5   **3.** $^{-}2\frac{2}{3}$

4. What is the sum of a number and its opposite?

ACE   Homework starts on page 16.

In golf, scores can be negative. Each golf hole has a value called par. Par is the number of strokes a golfer usually needs to complete the hole. For example, a good golfer, like Vijay Singh, should be able to complete a par 4 hole in four strokes. If a golfer completes the hole in six strokes, then his or her score for that hole is "two over par" ($^+2$). If a golfer completes the hole in two strokes, his or her score is "two under par" ($^-2$). A player's score for a round of golf is the total of the number of strokes above or under par.

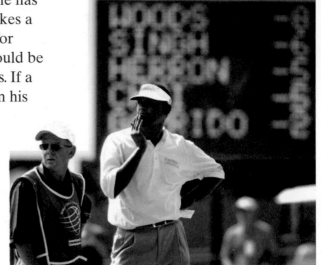

Go Online
PHSchool.com **For:** Information about golf
Web Code: ane-9031

1.3 What's the Change?

The National Weather Service keeps records of temperature changes.

The world record for fastest rise in outside air temperature occurred in Spearfish, South Dakota, on January 22, 1943. The temperature rose from $^-4°F$ to 45°F in two minutes.

What was the change in temperature over that two minutes? How could you show this change, n, on the number line?

From $^-4°F$ to 0°F is a change of $^+4°F$, and from 0°F to 45°F is a change of $^+45°F$. So the total change is $^+49°F$. The following number sentences show this.

$$^-4 + n = {}^+45$$
$$^-4 + {}^+49 = {}^+45$$

The sign of the change in temperature shows the direction of the change. In this case, $^+49$ means the temperature increased 49°F.

If the temperature had instead dropped 10° from ⁻4°F, you would write the change as ⁻10°F.

$$^-4 + {^-}10 = n$$
$$^-4 + {^-}10 = {^-}14$$

Problem 1.3 Using a Number Line Model

Sketch number lines and write number sentences for each question.

A. A person goes from a sauna at 120°F to an outside temperature of ⁻20°F. What is the change in temperature?

B. The temperature reading on a thermometer is 25°F. In the problems below, a positive number means the temperature is rising. A negative number means the temperature is falling. What is the new reading for each temperature change below?

    1. ⁺10°F   **2.** ⁻2°F   **3.** ⁻30°F

C. The temperature reading on a thermometer is ⁻15°F. What is the new reading for each temperature change?

    1. ⁺3°F   **2.** ⁻10°F   **3.** ⁺40°F

D. What is the change in temperature when the thermometer reading moves from the first temperature to the second temperature? Write an equation for each part.

    1. 20°F to ⁻10°F   **2.** ⁻20°F to ⁻10°F

    3. ⁻20°F to 10°F   **4.** ⁻10°F to ⁻20°F

    5. 20°F to 10°F   **6.** 10°F to 20°F

E. The temperature was ⁻5°F when Sally went to school on Monday. The temperature rose 20°F during the day, but fell 25°F during the night. A heat wave the next day increased the temperature 40°F. But an arctic wind overnight decreased the temperature 70°F! What was the temperature after the 70° decrease?

ACE   **Homework starts on page 16.**

1.4 In the Chips

When business records were kept by hand, accountants used red ink for expenses and black ink for income. If your income was greater than your expenses you were "in the black." If your expenses were greater than your income you were "in the red."

Julia has this problem to solve:

> Linda owes her sister $6 for helping her cut the lawn. She earns $4 delivering papers with her brother. Is she "in the red" or "in the black"?

Getting Ready for Problem 1.4

Julia uses red and black chips to model income and expenses. Each black chip represents $^+1$ dollar of income. Each red chip represents $^-1$ dollar of income (expenses).

Julia puts chips on the board to represent the situation. She decides Linda is "in the red" 2 dollars, or $^-2$ dollars.

Julia's Chip Board

- Why do you think she concludes that $^-6 + {}^+4 = {}^-2$?
- What is another way to show $^-2$ on the board?

Find the missing part for each chip problem. What would be a number sentence for each problem?

	Start With	Rule	End With
1.	●●●	Add 5 ●	■
2.	●●●	Subtract 3 ●	■
3.	●●● ●●●	■	●●
4.	■	Subtract 3 ●	●●●●

Problem 1.4 Using a Chip Model

Use ideas about black and red chips to answer each question. Then write a number sentence.

A. Give three combinations of red and black chips (using at least one of each color) that will equal each value.

    1. 0 **2.** $^+12$ **3.** $^-7$ **4.** $^-125$

B. Use this chip board as the starting value for each part. Find the total value on each chip board.

    1. original chip board

    2. add 5 black chips

    3. remove 5 red chips

    4. remove 3 black chips

    5. add 3 red chips

C. Cybil owes her sister $7. Her aunt pays her $5 to walk her dog. How much money does she have after she pays her sister?

D. Tate earns $10 mowing a lawn. He needs to pay $15 to rent his equipment. How much more money does he need to pay his rent?

active math online

For: Interactive Chip Model
Visit: PHSchool.com
Web Code: and-4104

E. Describe chip board displays that would match these number sentences. Find the results in each case.

    1. $^+3 - {^+2} = $ ■   **2.** $^-4 - {^+2} = $ ■   **3.** $^-4 - {^-2} = $ ■

    4. $^+7 + $ ■ $ = {^+1}$ **5.** $^-3 - {^+5} = $ ■   **6.** ■ $ - {^-2} = {^+6}$

ACE Homework starts on page 16.

Applications

Describe a sequence of five correct or incorrect answers that would produce each Math Fever score.

1. Super Brains: 300

2. Rocket Scientists: ⁻200

3. Know-It-Alls: ⁻250

4. Teacher's Pets: 0

5. Multiple Choice Which order is from least to greatest?

A. 300, 0, ⁻200, ⁻250

B. ⁻250, ⁻200, 0, 300

C. 0, ⁻200, ⁻250, 300

D. ⁻200, ⁻250, 300, 0

Find each Math Fever team's score. Write number sentences for each team. Assume that each team starts with 0 points.

6. Protons

Point Value	Answer
250	Correct
100	Correct
200	Correct
150	Incorrect
200	Incorrect

7. Neutrons

Point Value	Answer
200	Incorrect
50	Correct
250	Correct
150	Incorrect
50	Incorrect

8. Electrons

Point Value	Answer
50	Incorrect
200	Incorrect
100	Correct
200	Correct
150	Incorrect

For each set of rational numbers in Exercises 9 and 10, draw a number line and locate the points. Remember to choose an appropriate scale.

9. $\frac{-2}{8}$, $\frac{1}{4}$, ⁻1.5, $1\frac{3}{4}$

10. ⁻1.25, $\frac{-1}{3}$, 1.5, $\frac{-1}{6}$

11. Order the numbers from least to greatest.

23.6 ⁻45.2 50 ⁻0.5 0.3 $\frac{3}{5}$ $\frac{-4}{5}$

Homework Help Online
PHSchool.com
For: Help with Exercise 11
Web Code: ane-4111

Copy each pair of numbers in Exercises 12–19. Insert <, >, or = to make a true statement.

12. 3 ☐ 0

13. ⁻23.4 ☐ 23.4

14. 46 ☐ ⁻79

15. ⁻75 ☐ ⁻90

16. ⁻300 ☐ 100

17. ⁻1,000 ☐ ⁻999

18. ⁻1.73 ☐ ⁻1.730

19. ⁻4.3 ☐ ⁻4.03

Go Online
PHSchool.com

For: Multiple-Choice Skills Practice
Web Code: ana-4154

For Exercises 20–29, follow the steps using the number line. What is the final position?

20. Start at 8. Add ⁻7.

21. Start at ⁻8. Add 10.

22. Start at ⁻3. Add ⁻5.

23. Start at 7. Add ⁻7.

24. Start at ⁻2. Add 12.

25. Start at 3. Subtract 5.

26. Start at ⁻2. Subtract 2.

27. Start at 4. Subtract 7.

28. Start at 0. Subtract 5.

29. Start at ⁻8. Subtract 3.

30. The greatest one-day temperature change in world records occurred at Browning, Montana (bordering Glacier National Park), from January 23–24 in 1916. The temperature fell from 44°F to ⁻56°F in less than 24 hours.

   a. What was the temperature change that day?

   b. Write a number sentence to represent the temperature change.

   c. Show the temperature change on a number line.

Investigation 1 Extending the Number System   **17**

31. Find the value for each labeled point on the number line. Then use the values to calculate each change.

    a. A to B   **b.** A to C   **c.** B to C   **d.** C to A   **e.** B to A

Find the missing part for each situation.

	Start With	Rule	End With
32.	● ● ●	Add 5 ●	▪
33.	● ● ●	Subtract 3 ●	▪
34.	● ● ● ● ●	▪	● ●
35.	▪	Subtract 3 ●	● ● ● ● ●

36. Write a story problem for this situation. Find the value represented by the chips on the board.

For Exercises 37 and 38, use the chip board in Exercise 36.

37. Describe three different ways to change the numbers of black and red chips, but leave the value of the board unchanged.

38. Start with the original board. What is the new value of chips on the board when you

    a. remove 3 red chips?

    b. and then add 3 black chips?

    c. and then add 200 black chips and 195 red chips?

Connections

39. In a football game, one team makes seven plays in the first quarter. The results of those plays are (in order): gain of 7 yards, gain of 2 yards, loss of 5 yards, loss of 12 yards, gain of 16 yards, gain of 8 yards, loss of 8 yards.

   a. What is the overall gain (or loss) from all seven plays?

   b. What is the average gain (or loss) per play?

Find the number of strokes above or under par for each player. See the Did You Know? before the introduction to Problem 1.3 for the definition of par. Write number sentences with positive and negative numbers to show each result.

	Player	Round 1	Round 2	Round 3	Round 4
40.	Tiger Woods	4 over par	6 under par	3 under par	1 over par
41.	Karrie Webb	2 under par	1 under par	5 over par	5 under par

For Exercises 42 and 43, use the following information. The highest point on earth is the top of Mount Everest. It is 29,035 feet above sea level. The lowest exposed land is the shore of the Dead Sea. It is 1,310 feet below sea level.

42. Multiple Choice What is the change in elevation from the top of Everest to the shore of the Dead Sea?

   F. ⁻30,345 feet   **G.** ⁻27,725 feet

   H. 27,725 feet   **J.** 30,345 feet

43. Multiple Choice What is the change in elevation from the shore of the Dead Sea to the top of Everest?

   A. ⁻30,345 feet   **B.** ⁻27,725 feet

   C. 27,725 feet   **D.** 30,345 feet

Order the numbers from least to greatest.

44. $\frac{2}{5}, \quad \frac{3}{10}, \quad \frac{5}{9}, \quad \frac{9}{25}$ **45.** 20.33,   2.505,   23.30,   23

46. 1.52, $1\frac{4}{7}$,   2, $\frac{9}{6}$ **47.** 3, $\frac{19}{6}$, $2\frac{8}{9}$,   2.95

Extensions

48. At the start of December, Kenji had a balance of $595.50 in his checking account. The following is a list of transactions he made during the month.

Date	Transaction	Balance
December 1		$595.50
December 5	Writes a check for $19.95	
December 12	Writes a check for $280.88	
December 15	Deposits $257.00	
December 17	Writes a check for $58.12	
December 21	Withdraws $50.00	
December 24	Writes checks for $17.50, $41.37, and $65.15	
December 26	Deposits $100.00	
December 31	Withdraws $50.00	

   a. Copy and complete the table.

   b. What was Kenji's balance at the end of December?

   c. When was his balance the greatest?

   d. When was his balance the least?

Find the missing temperature information in each situation.

49. The high temperature is 20°C. The low temperature is ⁻15°C. What temperature is halfway between the high and the low?

50. The low temperature is ⁻8°C. The temperature halfway between the high and the low is 5°C. What is the high temperature?

51. The high temperature is ⁻10°C. The low temperature is ⁻15°C. What is the temperature halfway between the high and the low?

Find values for A and B that make each mathematical sentence true.

52. $^+A + {}^-B = {}^-1$

53. $^-A + {}^+B = 0$

54. $^-A - {}^-B = {}^-2$

Mathematical Reflections 1

In this investigation, you learned ways to order and operate with positive and negative numbers. The following questions will help you summarize what you have learned.

Think about your answers to these questions. Discuss your ideas with other students and your teacher. Then write a summary of your findings in your notebook.

1. How do you decide which of two numbers is greater when
   a. both numbers are positive?
   b. both numbers are negative?
   c. one number is positive and one number is negative?

2. What does comparing locations of numbers on a number line tell you about the numbers?

Investigation **2**

Adding and Subtracting Integers

In Investigation 1, you used number lines and chip boards to model operations with integers. Now, you will develop algorithms for adding and subtracting integers.

An **algorithm** is a plan, or series of steps, for doing a computation. In an effective algorithm, the steps lead to the correct answer, no matter what numbers you use. You may even develop more than one algorithm for each computation. Your goal should be to understand and skillfully use at least one algorithm for adding integers and at least one algorithm for subtracting integers.

2.1 Introducing Addition of Integers

There are two common ways that number problems lead to addition calculations like 8 + 5. The first involves combining two similar sets of objects, like in this example:

> John has 8 video games and his friend has 5. Together they have 8 + 5 = 13 games.

You can represent this situation on a chip board.

8 + 5 = 13

Number problems also lead to addition calculations when you add to a starting number. Take the following example:

> At a desert weather station, the temperature at sunrise was 10°C. It rose 25°C by noon. The temperature at noon was 10°C + 25°C = 35°C.

You can represent this situation on a number line. The starting point is $^+10$. The change in distance and direction is $^+25$. The sum ($^+35$) is the result of moving that distance and direction.

Suppose, instead of rising 25°C, the temperature fell 15°C. The next number line shows that $^+10°C + {}^-15°C = {}^-5°C$.

Use these ideas about addition as you develop an algorithm for addition of integers.

Problem 2.1 Introducing Addition of Integers

Use chip models or number line models.

A. 1. Find the sums in each group.

    2. Describe what the examples in each group have in common.

    3. Use your answer to part (2) to write two problems for each group.

    4. Describe an algorithm for adding integers in each group.

Group 1	Group 2
$^+2 + {}^+8$	$^+8 + {}^-12$
$^-3 + {}^-8$	$^-3 + {}^+2$
$^+20 + {}^+25$	$^+14 + {}^-23$
$^-24 + {}^-12$	$^-11 + {}^+13$

B. Write each number as a sum of integers in three different ways.

    1. $^-5$ **2.** $^+15$ **3.** 0

    4. Check to see whether your strategy for addition of integers works on these rational number problems.

        a. $^-1 + {}^+9$ **b.** $^-1\frac{1}{2} + {}^-\frac{3}{4}$ **c.** $^+1\frac{1}{2} + {}^-2\frac{3}{4}$

C. Write a story to match each number sentence. Find the solutions.

    1. $^+50 + {}^-65 = \blacksquare$ **2.** $^-15 + \blacksquare = {}^-25$ **3.** $^-300 + {}^-250 = \blacksquare$

D. Find both sums in parts (1) and (2). What do you notice?

    1. $^+12 + {}^-35$ $^-35 + {}^+12$ **2.** $^-7\frac{2}{3} + {}^-1\frac{1}{6}$ $^-1\frac{1}{6} + {}^-7\frac{2}{3}$

    3. The property of rational numbers that you have observed is called the **Commutative Property** of addition. What do you think the Commutative Property says about addition of rational numbers?

ACE Homework starts on page 32.

2.2 Introducing Subtraction of Integers

In some subtraction problems, you *take away* objects from a set, as in this first example:

> **Example 1** Kim had 9 CDs. She sold 4 CDs at a yard sale. She now has only $9 - 4 = 5$ of those CDs left.

You can represent this situation on a chip board.

$$9 - 4 = 5$$

Here is another example.

Example 2 Otis earned $5 babysitting. He owes Latoya $7. He pays her the $5. Represent this integer subtraction on a chip board.

To subtract 7 from 5 ($^+5 - {}^+7$), start by showing $^+5$ as black chips.

You can't take away $^+7$ because there aren't seven black chips to remove. Since adding both a red chip and a black chip does not change the value of the board, add two black chips and two red chips. The value of the board stays the same, but now there are 7 black chips to take away.

$$5 - 7 = {}^-2$$

What is left on the board when you take away the 7 black chips?

The changes on the board can be represented by $(^-2 + 2) + 5 - 7 = {}^-2$. Otis now has $^-$2. He still owes Latoya $2.

In a third example of a subtraction problem, you find the *difference* between two numbers.

Example 3 The Arroyo family just passed mile 25 on the highway. They need to get to the exit at mile 80. How many more miles do they have to drive?

You can use a number line to show differences.

The arrow on the number line points in the direction of travel. The Arroyos are traveling in a positive direction from small values to greater values. They still have to travel $80 - 25 = 55$ miles.

If the Arroyos drive back from mile 80 to mile 25, they still have to travel 55 miles. This time, however, they travel in the opposite direction. The number sentence $25 - 80 = {}^-55$ represents this situation.

Now, the arrow points to the left and has a label of $^-55$. The distance is 55, but the direction is negative.

Sometimes you only want the distance and not direction. You can show distance by putting vertical bars around the given number. This is called absolute value. The **absolute value** of a number is its distance from 0 on the number line.

$$|^-55| = 55 \qquad |^+55| = 55$$

You say "the absolute value of $^-55$ is 55" and "the absolute value of $^+55$ is 55."

When you write a number and a sign (or an implied sign for $+$) on an arrow above a number line, you are indicating both distance and direction.

In a problem that involves the amount of money you have and the amount that you owe, is the sign (direction) important?

Problem 2.2 Introducing Subtraction of Integers

Use chip models or number line models.

A. 1. Find the differences in each group below.

Group 1
$^+12 - \,^+8$
$^-5 - \,^-7$
$^-4 - \,^-2$
$^+2 - \,^+4$

Group 2
$^+12 - \,^-8$
$^-5 - \,^+7$
$^-4 - \,^+2$
$^+2 - \,^-4$

 2. Describe what the examples in each group have in common.

 3. Use your answer to part (2) to write two problems for each group.

 4. Describe an algorithm for subtracting integers in each group.

 5. Check to see whether your strategy for subtraction of integers works on these rational number problems:

   a. $^-1 - \,^+3$ **b.** $^-1 - \,^+\frac{3}{4}$

   c. $^-1\frac{1}{2} - \,^-2$ **d.** $^-1\frac{1}{2} - \,^-\frac{3}{4}$

B. Write each number as a difference of integers in three different ways.

 1. $^-5$ **2.** $^+15$

 3. 0 **4.** $^-3.5$

C. For parts (1)–(4), decide whether the expressions are equal.

 1. $^-2 - \,^+3 \stackrel{?}{=} \,^+3 - \,^-2$ **2.** $^+12 - \,^-4 \stackrel{?}{=} \,^-4 - \,^+12$

 3. $^-15 - \,^-20 \stackrel{?}{=} \,^-20 - \,^-15$ **4.** $^+45 - \,^+21 \stackrel{?}{=} \,^+21 - \,^+45$

 5. Do you think there is a Commutative Property of subtraction?

ACE **Homework starts on page 32.**

2.3 The "+/−" Connection

You have probably noticed that addition and subtraction are related to each other. You can write any addition sentence as an equivalent subtraction sentence. You can also write any subtraction sentence as an equivalent addition sentence.

Getting Ready for Problem 2.3

The chip board below shows a value of $^+5$.

- There are two possible moves, one addition and one subtraction, that would change the value on the board to $^+2$ in one step. How would you complete the number sentences to represent each move?

$$^+5 + \blacksquare = {}^+2 \text{ and } {}^+5 - \blacksquare = {}^+2$$

- There are two possible moves, one addition and one subtraction, that would change the value on the board to $^+8$ in one step. How would you complete the number sentences to represent each move?

$$^+5 + \blacksquare = {}^+8 \text{ and } {}^+5 - \blacksquare = {}^+8$$

- Can you describe a general relationship between addition and subtraction for integers?

Use your ideas about addition and subtraction of integers to explore the relationship between these two operations.

A. Complete each number sentence.

1. $^+5 + {}^-2 = {}^+5 - \blacksquare$

2. $^+5 + {}^+4 = {}^+5 - \blacksquare$

3. $^-7 + {}^-2 = {}^-7 - \blacksquare$

4. $^-7 + {}^+2 = {}^-7 - \blacksquare$

B. What patterns do you see in the results of Question A that suggest a way to restate any addition problem as an equivalent subtraction problem?

C. Complete each number sentence.

1. $^+8 - {}^+5 = 8 + \blacksquare$

2. $^+8 - {}^-5 = 8 + \blacksquare$

3. $^-4 - {}^+6 = {}^-4 + \blacksquare$

4. $^-4 - {}^-6 = {}^-4 + \blacksquare$

D. What patterns do you see in the results of Question C that suggest a way to restate any subtraction problem as an equivalent addition problem?

E. Write an equivalent problem for each. Then find the results.

1. $^+396 - {}^-400$

2. $^-75.8 - {}^-35.2$

3. $^-25.6 + {}^-4.4$

4. $^+\frac{3}{2} - {}^+\frac{1}{4}$

5. $^+\frac{5}{8} + {}^-\frac{3}{4}$

6. $^-3\frac{1}{2} - {}^+5$

ACE Homework starts on page 32.

2.4 Fact Families

You can rewrite $3 + 2 = 5$ to make a fact family that shows how the addition sentence is related to two subtraction sentences.

$$3 + 2 = 5$$
$$2 + 3 = 5$$
$$5 - 3 = 2$$
$$5 - 2 = 3$$

Problem 2.4 Fact Families

A. Write a related subtraction fact for each.

   1. $^-3 + {}^-2 = {}^-5$ **2.** $^+25 + {}^-32 = {}^-7$

B. Write a related addition fact for each.

   1. $^+8 - {}^-2 = {}^+10$ **2.** $^-14 - {}^-20 = 6$

C. 1. Write a related sentence for each.

   a. $n - {}^+5 = {}^+35$ **b.** $n - {}^-5 = {}^+35$ **c.** $n + {}^+5 = {}^+35$

  2. Do your related sentences make it easier to find the value for n? Why or why not?

D. 1. Write a related sentence for each.

   a. $^+4 + n = {}^+43$ **b.** $^-4 + n = {}^+43$ **c.** $^-4 + n = {}^-43$

  2. Do your related sentences make it easier to find the value for n? Why or why not?

ACE Homework starts on page 32.

2.5 Coordinate Graphing

In your study of similar figures, you used positive number coordinates and arithmetic operations to locate and move points and figures around a coordinate grid. You can use negative number coordinates to produce a grid that extends in all directions.

Coordinate Plane

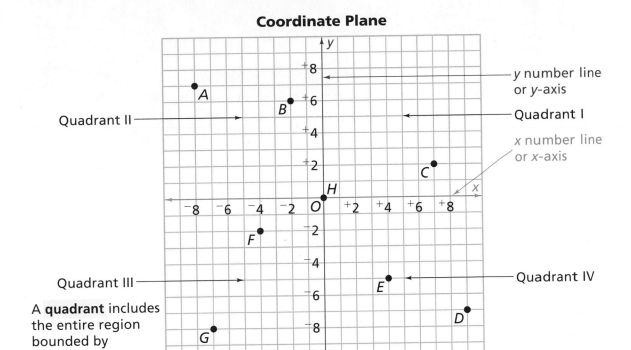

Problem 2.5 Coordinate Graphing

A. Write the coordinates for each point labeled with a letter.

B. What is the sign of the *x*-value and the *y*-value for any point in Quadrant I? Quadrant II? Quadrant III? Quadrant IV?

C. The point "opposite" ($^-5$, $^+8$) has coordinates ($^+5$, $^-8$). Notice that the sign of each coordinate in the pair changes. Write the coordinates for the points "opposite" the labeled points. On a grid like the one shown, graph and label each "opposite" point with a letter followed by a tick mark. Point A′ is "opposite" point A.

D. Draw line segments connecting each pair of related points (A and A′, B and B′, etc.). What do you notice about the line segments?

E. Plot the points in each part on a grid. Connect the points to form a triangle. Draw each triangle in a different color, but on the same grid.

    1. ($^+1$, $^-1$)   ($^+2$, $^+3$)   ($^-4$, $^-2$)

    2. ($^-1$, $^-1$)   ($^-2$, $^+3$)   ($^+4$, $^-2$)

    3. ($^-1$, $^+1$)   ($^-2$, $^-3$)   ($^+4$, $^+2$)

    4. ($^+1$, $^+1$)   (2, $^-3$)   ($^-4$, $^+2$)

    5. How is triangle 1 related to triangle 2? How is triangle 1 related to triangle 3? To triangle 4?

ACE Homework starts on page 32.

Applications

1. Use your algorithms to find each sum without using a calculator.

   a. $^+12 + {}^+4$ **b.** $^+12 + {}^-4$ **c.** $^-12 + {}^+4$

   d. $^-7 + {}^-8$ **e.** $^+4.5 + {}^-3.8$ **f.** $^-4.5 + {}^+3.8$

   g. $^-250 + {}^-750$ **h.** $^-6{,}200 + {}^+1{,}200$ **i.** $^+0.75 + {}^-0.25$

   j. $^+\frac{2}{3} + {}^-\frac{1}{6}$ **k.** $^-\frac{5}{12} + {}^+\frac{2}{3}$ **l.** $^-\frac{8}{5} + {}^-\frac{3}{5}$

2. Find each sum.

   a. $^+3.8 + {}^+2.7$ **b.** $^-3.8 + {}^-2.7$

   c. $^-3.8 + {}^+2.7$ **d.** $^+3.8 + {}^-2.7$

3. Write an addition number sentence that matches each diagram.

   a.

   b.

   c.

   d.

The chip board has 10 black and 13 red chips. Use the chip board for Exercises 4 and 5.

4. What is the value shown on the board?

5. Write a number sentence to represent each situation. Then find the new value of the chip board.

    a. Remove 5 red chips from the original board.

    b. Then add 5 black chips.

    c. Then add 4 black chips and 4 red chips.

6. Use your algorithms to find each difference without using a calculator. Show your work.

    a. $^+12 - {}^+4$ **b.** $^+4 - {}^+12$ **c.** $^-12 - {}^+4$

    d. $^-7 - {}^+8$ **e.** $^+45 - {}^-40$ **f.** $^+45 - {}^-50$

    g. $^-25 - {}^-75$ **h.** $^-62 - {}^-12$ **i.** $^+0.8 - {}^-0.5$

    j. $^+\frac{1}{2} - {}^+\frac{3}{4}$ **k.** $^-\frac{2}{5} - {}^+\frac{1}{5}$ **l.** $^-\frac{7}{10} - {}^+\frac{4}{5}$

Go Online
PHSchool.com
For: Multiple-Choice Skills Practice
Web Code: ana-4254

7. Find each value without using a calculator.

    a. $^+12 + {}^-12$ **b.** $^+12 - {}^+12$ **c.** $^-12 - {}^+12$

    d. $^-12 - {}^-12$ **e.** $^-12 + {}^-12$ **f.** $^-12 + {}^+12$

8. Find each value.

    a. $^+50 + {}^-35$ **b.** $^+50 - {}^-20$ **c.** $^-19 - {}^+11$

    d. $^-30 - {}^+50$ **e.** $^-35 + {}^-15$ **f.** $^+12 + {}^-18$

9. Write a story about temperature, money, or game scores to represent each number sentence.

   a. $^+7 - ^-4 = ^+11$ b. $^-20 + ^+n = ^+30$ c. $^-n + ^-150 = ^-350$

10. Without doing any calculations, decide which will give the greater result. Explain your reasoning.

    a. $^+5,280 + ^-768$ OR $^+5,280 - ^-768$
    b. $^+1,760 - ^-880$ OR $^+1,760 - ^+880$
    c. $^+1,500 + ^+3,141$ OR $^+1,500 - ^-3,141$

11. Without doing any calculations, determine whether each result is positive or negative. Explain.

    a. $^-23 + ^+19$ b. $^+3.5 - ^-2.7$
    c. $^-3.5 - ^-2.04$ d. $^+3.1 + ^-6.2$

12. Find each missing part.

	Start With	Rule	End With
a.	●●	▪	●●●●●●●
b.	●●●	▪	●●●
c.	⊘ ⊘	Add 5 ●	●●●
d.	⊘ ⊘ ⊘ ⊘ ⊘	Subtract 5 ●	●●

13. Find each sum or difference. Show your work.

    a. $^+15 + ^-10$ b. $^-20 - ^+14$
    c. $^+200 - ^-125$ d. $^-20 - ^-14$
    e. $^-200 + ^+125$ f. $^+7 - ^+12$

14. Below is part of a time line with three years marked.

1986   1996   2006

    a. How does 1996 relate to 1986? How does 1996 relate to 2006?

    b. Write two number sentences. One must relate 1996 to 1986. The other must relate 1996 to 2006.

    c. How are these two number sentences alike and different?

15. Compute each value.

    a. $^{+}3 + {}^{-}3 + {}^{-}7$ **b.** $^{+}3 - {}^{+}3 - {}^{+}7$

    c. $^{-}10 + {}^{-}7 + {}^{-}28$ **d.** $^{-}10 - {}^{+}7 - {}^{+}28$

    e. $7 - {}^{+}8 + {}^{-}5$ **f.** $^{+}7 + {}^{-}8 - {}^{+}5$

    g. $^{-}97 + {}^{-}35 - {}^{+}10$ **h.** $^{-}97 - {}^{+}35 + {}^{-}10$

    i. What can you conclude about the relationship between subtracting a positive number $(-\ ^{+})$ and adding a negative number $(+\ ^{-})$ with the same absolute value?

16. Compute each value.

    a. $^{+}3 - {}^{-}3 - {}^{-}7$ **b.** $^{+}3 + {}^{+}3 + {}^{+}7$

    c. $^{-}10 - {}^{-}7 - {}^{-}28$ **d.** $^{-}10 + {}^{+}7 + {}^{+}28$

    e. $^{+}7 + {}^{+}8 + {}^{+}5$ **f.** $^{+}7 - {}^{-}8 - {}^{-}5$

    g. $^{-}97 - {}^{-}35 - {}^{+}10$ **h.** $^{-}97 + {}^{+}35 + {}^{-}10$

    i. What can you conclude about the relationship between subtracting a negative number $(-\ ^{-})$ and adding a positive number $(+\ ^{+})$ with the same absolute value?

Multiple Choice In each set of calculations, one result is different from the others. Find the different result without doing any calculations.

17. A. $54 + {}^{-}25$ **B.** $54 - 25$

    C. $25 - 54$ **D.** $^{-}25 + 54$

18. F. $^{-}6.28 - {}^{-}3.14$ **G.** $^{-}6.28 + 3.14$

    H. $3.14 + {}^{-}6.28$ **J.** $^{-}3.14 - {}^{-}6.28$

19. A. $534 - 275$ **B.** $275 - 534$

    C. $^{-}534 + 275$ **D.** $275 + {}^{-}534$

20. F. $175 + {}^{-}225$ **G.** $225 - 175$

    H. $175 - 225$ **J.** $^{-}225 + 175$

21. Fill in the missing information for each problem.

a. $^+5 + ^-\frac{3}{4} = \blacksquare$ **b.** $^+\frac{4}{8} + ^-6 = \blacksquare$ **c.** $^-3\frac{3}{4} - ^-\frac{3}{4} = \blacksquare$

d. $^+2\frac{2}{3} - ^+\frac{1}{3} = \blacksquare$ **e.** $^-2 + \blacksquare = ^-2\frac{1}{2}$ **f.** $^-4.5 + \blacksquare = ^-5$

22. Multiple Choice Which is the correct addition and subtraction fact family for $^-2 + ^+3 = ^+1$?

A. $^-2 + 3 = 1$
$\quad ^-2 + 1 = 3$
$\quad 3 - 1 = 2$

B. $^-2 + ^+3 = ^+1$
$\quad ^-2 + 3 = 1$
$\quad 3 - 1 = 2$

C. $^-2 + 3 = 1$
$\quad 1 - 3 = ^-2$
$\quad 1 - ^-2 = 3$

D. $\quad 1 - 3 = ^-2$
$\quad 1 - ^-2 = 3$
$\quad 3 - 1 = 2$

23. Write a related fact for each number sentence to find n. What is the value of n?

a. $n - ^+7 = ^+10$ **b.** $\frac{-1}{2} + n = \frac{-5}{8}$ **c.** $^+\frac{2}{3} - n = \frac{-7}{9}$

24. Are $^+8 - ^+8$ and $8 - 8$ equivalent? Explain.

25. Are $^+100 - ^+99$ and $100 - 99$ equivalent? Explain.

26. Are the expressions in each group below equivalent? If so, which form makes the computation easiest?

a. $^+8 + ^-10$
$\quad 8 - ^+10$
$\quad 8 - 10$

b. $3 + ^-8$
$\quad 3 - ^+8$
$\quad 3 - 8$

27. Locate each pair of points on a coordinate grid. Describe the direction from the first point to the second point. Use these descriptions: to the left, to the right, downward, and upward.

a. $(^+3, ^+2); (^-5, ^+2)$ **b.** $(^-7, ^+7); (^+3, ^+7)$ **c.** $(^-8, ^-2); (^+4, ^-2)$

d. $(^+4, ^+4); (^+4, ^+20)$ **e.** $(^+18, ^+8); (^+18, ^-8)$ **f.** $(^-20, ^-4); (^-20, ^+9)$

g. Movement to the right or upward is in a positive direction. Movement to the left or downward is in a negative direction. Explain why this makes sense.

h. Now, describe the direction and the distance between the first point and the second point. For example, an answer of $^-15$ means you move in a negative direction a distance of 15. Whether the change is in the x-coordinate or the y-coordinate will tell whether $^-15$ means down 15 or to the left 15.

28. a. Locate three points on a coordinate grid that could be the vertices of a right triangle.

b. Find two different points that make a right triangle with coordinates ($^-$2, $^+$2) and ($^+$3, $^+$1).

For: Help with Exercise 28
Web Code: ane-4228

29. Find the opposite of each point in the graph. [Remember, the opposite of ($^+$2, $^-$1) is ($^-$2, $^+$1).]

a.
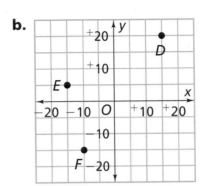

b.

Connections

30. The Spartan Bike Shop keeps a record of their business transactions. They start their account at zero dollars. Payments represent negative transactions. Sales represent positive transactions. Write a number sentence to represent each transaction. Then find the new balance.

a. rent payment for shop: $1,800

b. payment for 20 new bicycles: $2,150

c. payment on office equipment: $675

d. business insurance for 6 months: $2,300

e. sale of 3 bicycles: $665

f. sale of two helmets and one baby seat: $95

g. Web site advertising down payment: $250

h. sale of 6 bicycles: $1,150

i. refund to an unhappy customer: $225

j. sale of 2 bicycles, two helmets, and two air pumps: $750

k. check from manufacturer for 5 bicycles returned: $530

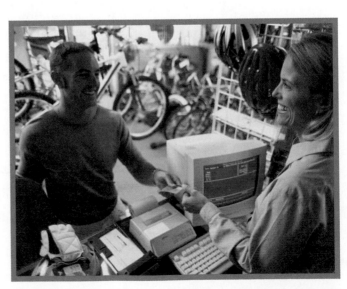

Investigation 2 Adding and Subtracting Integers **37**

Write a number sentence for each situation in Exercises 31 and 32.

31. The air temperature drops from 94° to 72° in 15 minutes. What is the change in temperature?

32. The Teacher's Pets team has 50 points in MathMania. They miss a 200-point question. What is their new score?

33. Find four different numbers, in order from least to greatest, that lie between the two given numbers.

    a. ⁻4.5 and ⁻3.5   **b.** ⁻0.5 and ⁺0.5

34. The diagram below shows Mug Wump drawn at the center of a coordinate grid and in four other positions.

    a. Find a sequence of coordinates to draw Mug's body at the center of the grid. Make a table to keep track of the points.

    b. You can write a coordinate rule to describe the movement of points from one location to another. For example, the coordinate rule $(x, y) \rightarrow (x - {}^+2, y + {}^+3)$ moves a point (x, y) to the left 2 units and up 3 units from its original location. The coordinate rule $(x, y) \rightarrow (x + {}^+6, y - {}^+7)$ moves points of the original Mug to produce which of the other drawings?

    c. Find coordinate rules for moving the original Mug to the other positions on the grid.

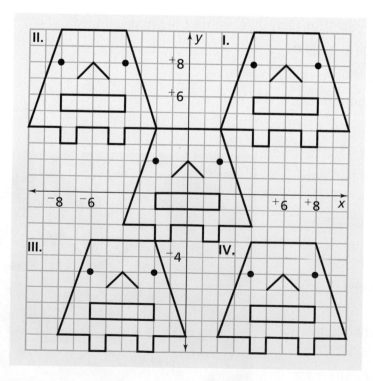

Use the points in each coordinate grid to determine what scale interval was used on each axis.

35.

36.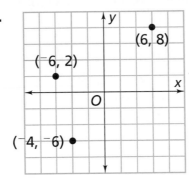

Extensions

37. Which numbers, when added to $^-15$, give a sum

    a. greater than 0   **b.** less than 0   **c.** equal to 0

38. Find the distance between each pair of numbers on a number line.

    a. $^+8, ^+4$ **b.** $^-8, ^+4$ **c.** $^+8, ^-4$

    d. $^-8, ^-4$ **e.** $^-3\frac{1}{2}, ^+\frac{3}{4}$ **f.** $^+5.4, ^-1.6$

39. Find each absolute value.

    a. $|^+8 - ^+4|$ **b.** $|^-8 - ^+4|$ **c.** $|^+8 - ^-4|$

    d. $|^-8 - ^-4|$ **e.** $|^-3\frac{1}{2} + ^+\frac{3}{4}|$ **f.** $|^+5.4 - ^-1.6|$

    g. Compare the results of parts (a)–(f) with the distances found in Exercise 38. What do you notice? Why do you think this is so?

40. Replace n with a number to make each statement true.

    a. $n + ^-18 = ^+6$ **b.** $^-24 - n = ^+12$

    c. $^+43 + n = ^-12$ **d.** $^-20 - n = ^-50$

41. The table shows the profits or losses (in millions of dollars) earned by three companies from 1997 to 2006. Find the range of the annual results and the overall profit (or loss) for each company over that time period.

	Company	'97	'98	'99	'00	'01	'02	'03	'04	'05	'06
a.	Sands Motor	⁻5.3	⁻4.8	⁻7.2	⁻2.1	1.4	6.5	3.2	⁻3.5	10.2	2.4
b.	Daily Trans	6.0	3.4	⁻5.8	⁻12.3	⁻20.3	⁻1.5	2.5	9.8	19.4	32.1
c.	Sell to You	120	98	⁻20	⁻40	⁻5	85	130	76	5	⁻30

42. Julia thinks a bit more about how to use red and black chips to model operations with integers. She draws the following chip board. She decides it represents $8 \times {}^-5 = {}^-40$ and $^-40 \div 8 = {}^-5$.

   a. Explain why Julia's reasoning makes sense.

   b. Use Julia's reasoning to find each value.

   i. $10 \times {}^-5$ **ii.** $4 \times {}^-15$ **iii.** $3 \times {}^-5$

   iv. $^-14 \div 2$ **v.** $^-14 \div 7$ **vi.** $^-35 \div 7$

43. Starting from 0, write an addition sentence for diagram below.

   a.

   b.

Mathematical Reflections 2

In this investigation, you applied your ideas about integers to develop algorithms for calculating any sums and differences.

Think about your answers to these questions. Discuss your ideas with other students and your teacher. Then write a summary of findings in your notebook.

1. **a.** How can you decide if the sum of two numbers is positive, negative, or zero without actually calculating the sum?

   b. How can you decide if the difference of two numbers is positive, negative, or zero without actually calculating the difference?

2. **a.** What procedure(s) will find the sum $a + b$ of two numbers where a and b represent any integer?

   b. What procedure(s) will find the difference $a - b$ of two numbers where a and b represent any integer?

3. How can any difference $a - b$ of two numbers be restated as an equivalent addition statement?

Multiplying and Dividing Integers

Some Notes on Notation

You have been writing integers with raised signs to avoid confusion with the symbols for addition and subtraction. However, most computer software and most writing in mathematics do not use raised signs.

Positive numbers are usually written without a sign.

$$^+3 = 3 \text{ and } ^+7.5 = 7.5$$

Negative numbers are usually written with a dash like a subtraction sign.

$$^-3 = -3 \text{ and } ^-7.5 = -7.5$$

From now on, we will use this notation to indicate a negative number.

This can be confusing if you don't read carefully. Parentheses can help.

$$^-5 - {}^-8 = -5 - -8 = -5 - (-8)$$

The subtraction symbol also indicates the opposite of a number. For example, -8 represents the opposite of 8. The expression $-(-8)$ represents the opposite of -8.

$$-(-8) = 8$$

For multiplication, you can use a raised dot symbol.

$$3 \times 5 = 3 \cdot 5$$

In this investigation, you will use time, distance, speed, and direction to think about multiplication and division of integers. You will also look at number patterns and develop algorithms for multiplying and dividing these numbers.

Michael Johnson set a world record by running 400 meters in 43.18 seconds at the world track championships in 1999. Florence Griffith Joyner set an Olympic record when she ran 100 meters in 10.62 seconds in 1988.

How long would it take each runner to run 1,000 meters at his or her record speed?

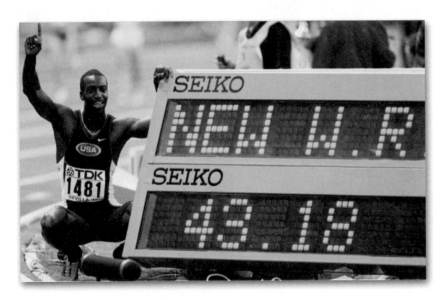

Go Online
PHSchool.com
For: Information about track
Web Code: ane-9031

The math department at Everett Middle School sponsors a contest called the Number Relay. A number line measured in meters is drawn on the school field. Each team has five runners. Runners 1, 3, and 5 stand at the −50 meter line. Runners 2 and 4 stand at the 50 meter line.

Team 1

For Team 1:

- Hahn starts and runs from −50 to 50. He tags Aurelia.
- Aurelia runs back from 50 to −50. She tags Dwayne.
- Dwayne runs from −50 to 50. He tags Tori.
- Tori runs from 50 to −50. She tags Pascal.
- Pascal runs from −50 to the finish line at position 0.

The team whose final runner reaches the 0 point first wins.

A. Write number sentences that express your answers to these questions. Use positive numbers for running speeds to the right and negative numbers for running speeds to the left. Use positive numbers for time in the future and negative numbers for time in the past. Each runner runs at a constant speed.

1. Hahn passes the 0 point running 5 meters per second to the right. Where is he 10 seconds later?

2. Dwayne passes the 0 point running 4 meters per second to the right. Where is he 5 seconds later?

3. Aurelia passes the 0 point running to the left at 6 meters per second. Where is she 8 seconds later?

4. Pascal passes the 0 point running to the right at 3 meters per second. Where was he 6 seconds earlier?

5. Tori passes the 0 point running to the left at 5 meters per second. Where was she 7 seconds earlier?

B. 1. Find the products in each group below.

Group 1	Group 2	Group 3
4×3	$4 \times (-3)$	$-4 \times (-3)$
5.1×1	-1.5×2	$-7 \times (-4)$
3×4.5	$10 \times (-11)$	$-5.2 \times (-1)$

2. Describe what the examples in each group have in common.

3. Use your answer to part (2) to write two problems for each group.

4. Describe an algorithm for multiplying rational numbers.

5. Use your strategy to multiply these rational numbers.
   a. $-1\frac{1}{2} \times \frac{3}{4}$ **b.** $-\frac{1}{2} \times \left(-\frac{3}{4}\right)$ **c.** $2\frac{1}{2} \times \left(-\frac{3}{4}\right)$

6. Is multiplication commutative? Does the order of factors matter? For example, are these multiplication sentences correct?

$$2 \cdot 3 \stackrel{?}{=} 3 \cdot 2$$
$$-2 \times (-3) \stackrel{?}{=} -3 \times (-2)$$
$$-2 \times 3 \stackrel{?}{=} 3 \times (-2)$$

ACE Homework starts on page 50.

3.2 Multiplication Patterns

After studying the relay race problem, some students started playing with number patterns to see whether what they found in the relay race made sense. Study the equations below. Look for patterns.

$$5 \times 5 = 25$$
$$5 \times 4 = 20$$
$$5 \times 3 = 15$$
$$5 \times 2 = 10$$
$$5 \times 1 = 5$$
$$5 \times 0 = 0$$

Problem 3.2 Multiplication Patterns

A. 1. How do the products change as the numbers multiplied by 5 get smaller?

2. Predict $5 \times (-1), 5 \times (-2)$, and $5 \times (-3)$. Explain your reasoning.

3. Write the next four equations in the pattern.

B. 1. Complete the equations below.

$$(-4) \times 5 = \blacksquare$$
$$(-4) \times 4 = \blacksquare$$
$$(-4) \times 3 = \blacksquare$$
$$(-4) \times 2 = \blacksquare$$
$$(-4) \times 1 = \blacksquare$$
$$(-4) \times 0 = \blacksquare$$

2. How do the products change as the numbers multiplied by -4 get smaller?

3. Predict $-4 \times (-1)$. Explain.

4. Write the next four equations in the pattern.

C. 1. Find each value.

    a. $7 \times (-8) \times (-3)$

    b. $-12 \times (-5) \times (-4)$

    c. $\frac{1}{2} \times \left(-\frac{2}{3}\right) \times 3$

2. How do the patterns you found in this problem compare to the algorithm from Problem 3.1?

ACE Homework starts on page 50.

3.3 Introducing Division of Integers

You know there is a relationship between addition and subtraction facts. A similar relationship exists between multiplication and division. For any multiplication fact, we can write another multiplication fact and two different related division facts. Here are three examples. $\left(\text{Remember that you can write } 15 \div 3 \text{ as a fraction, } \frac{15}{3}.\right)$

Example 1	Example 2	Example 3
$5 \times 3 = 15$	$6 \times (-3) = -18$	$4.5 \times (-2) = -9$
$3 \times 5 = 15$	$-3 \times 6 = -18$	$-2 \times 4.5 = -9$
$15 \div 3 = 5 \text{ or } \frac{15}{3} = 5$	$-18 \div (-3) = 6 \text{ or } \frac{-18}{-3} = 6$	$-9 \div (-2) = 4.5 \text{ or } \frac{-9}{-2} = 4.5$
$15 \div 5 = 3 \text{ or } \frac{15}{5} = 3$	$-18 \div 6 = -3 \text{ or } \frac{-18}{6} = -3$	$-9 \div 4.5 = -2 \text{ or } \frac{-9}{4.5} = -2$

Getting Ready for Problem 3.3

- What patterns do you see in Examples 1–3?
- Write a fact family for $-2 \times 3 = -6$.
- How can you use what you know about the relationship between multiplication and division facts to help you solve these problems?

  1. $8 \times \blacksquare = -48$

  2. $\blacksquare \times (-9) = 108$

  3. $6 \times (-13) = \blacksquare$

You can use this relationship and your ideas from the Number Relay questions to develop algorithms for dividing integers.

A. Recall the Number Relay from Problem 3.1. Write division sentences that express your answers to the questions below.

    1. Dwayne goes from 0 to 15 in 5 seconds. At what rate (distance per second) does he run?

    2. Aurelia reaches -12 only 3 seconds after passing 0. At what rate does she run to the left?

    3. Pascal passes 0 running to the right at a rate of 5 meters per second. When did he leave the point -50? When did he leave the point -24?

    4. Tori wants to reach the point -40 running to the left at 8 meters per second. How long will it take her from the time she passes 0?

B. **1.** Find the quotients in each group below.

Group 1	Group 2	Group 3
$12 \div 3$	$39 \div (-3)$	$-45 \div (-3)$
$51 \div 5$	$-15 \div 4$	$-4.8 \div (-4)$
$4.5 \div 9$	$10 \div (-5)$	$-72 \div (-12)$

    2. Describe what the examples in each group have in common.

    3. Use your answer to part (2) to write two problems for each group.

    4. Describe an algorithm for dividing rational numbers.

    5. Use your strategy to divide these rational numbers.

        a. $-1\frac{1}{2} \div \frac{3}{4}$ **b.** $-\frac{1}{2} \div \left(-\frac{3}{4}\right)$ **c.** $2\frac{1}{2} \div \left(-\frac{3}{4}\right)$

    6. Is division commutative? Does $-2 \div 3 = 3 \div (-2)$? Give two other examples to support your answer.

ACE Homework starts on page 50.

3.4 Playing the Integer Product Game

You have developed algorithms for multiplying and dividing integers. You will need them to play the Integer Product Game.

The game board consists of a list of factors and a grid of products. To play, you need a game board, two paper clips, and colored markers or chips.

Integer Product Game Rules

1. Player A puts a paper clip on a number in the factor list.
2. Player B puts the other paper clip on any number in the factor list, including the number chosen by Player A. Player B then marks the product of the two factors on the product grid.
3. Player A moves *either one* of the paper clips to another number. He or she then marks the new product with a different color than Player B.
4. Each player takes turns moving a paper clip and marking a product. A product can only be marked by one player.
5. The winner is the first player to mark four squares in a row (up and down, across, or diagonally).

Integer Product Game Board

–36	–30	–25	–24	–20	–18
–16	–15	–12	–10	–9	–8
–6	–5	–4	–3	–2	–1
1	2	3	4	5	6
8	9	10	12	15	16
18	20	24	25	30	36

Factors:

–6 –5 –4 –3 –2 –1 1 2 3 4 5 6

Problem 3.4 Multiplying Integers

Play the Integer Product Game with positive and negative factors. Look for strategies for picking the factors and products.

A. What strategies did you find useful in playing the game? Explain.

B. What pair(s) of numbers from the factor list will give each product?

   1. 5   **2.** −12   **3.** 12   **4.** −25

C. Your opponent puts a paper clip on −4. List five products that you can form. Tell where you need to put your paper clip in each case.

D. Describe the moves to make in each case.

   1. The paper clips are on −5 and −2. You want a product of −15.

   2. The paper clips are on −3 and −2. You want a product of −6.

   3. Your opponent will win with 24. What numbers should you avoid with your paper clip moves?

active math online

For: Integer Product Game Activity
Visit: PHSchool.com
Web Code: and-4304

ACE Homework starts on page 50.

Applications

1. At some international airports, trains carry passengers between the separate terminal buildings. Suppose that one such train system moves along a track like the one below.

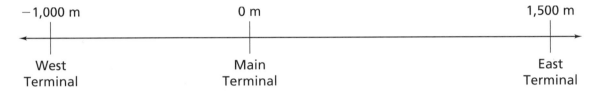

−1,000 m	0 m	1,500 m
West Terminal	Main Terminal	East Terminal

a. A train leaves the main terminal going east at 10 meters per second. Where will it be in 10 seconds? When will it reach the east terminal?

b. A train passes the main terminal going east at 10 meters per second. Where was that train 15 seconds ago? When was it at the west terminal?

c. A train leaves the main terminal going west at 10 meters per second. Where will it be in 20 seconds? When will it reach the west terminal?

d. A train passes the main terminal going west at 10 meters per second. When was it at the east terminal? Where was it 20 seconds ago?

The dot patterns illustrate commutative properties for operations on whole numbers. Write a number sentence for each case.

2.

3.

4. Find each value.

   a. $7 \cdot 2$ **b.** $-7 \times (-2)$ **c.** $7 \times (-2)$

   d. -7×2 **e.** $8 \cdot 2.5$ **f.** $-9 \times (-4)$

   g. $12 \times (-3)$ **h.** -1.5×4 **i.** 3.5×7

   j. $-8.1 \cdot (-1)$ **k.** $1 \times (-6)$ **l.** $-2\frac{1}{2} \times 1$

5. Find the values for each pair.

   a. $4 \times (-3)$ and -3×4 **b.** $2 \cdot (-4)$ and $-4 \cdot 2$

   c. $-2 \times (-3)$ and $-3 \times (-2)$ **d.** $\frac{1}{5} \times \left(-\frac{4}{9}\right)$ and $-\frac{4}{9} \times \frac{1}{5}$

   e. What can you conclude about multiplication with negative numbers?

6. Tell whether each product is greater than or less than zero.

   a. $5 \times (-7)$ **b.** $-3.2 \cdot 1.5$

   c. $10.5 \times (-4)$ **d.** $-2 \times (-3) \times (-1)$

   e. $-\frac{2}{3} \cdot 2\frac{3}{4}$ **f.** $-\frac{3}{4} \times \left(-1\frac{5}{6}\right) \times \left(-\frac{7}{4}\right)$

   g. $-\frac{3}{4} \times \left(-1\frac{5}{6}\right) \times \frac{7}{4}$ **h.** $-\frac{3}{4} \times \left(-1\frac{5}{6}\right) \times \left(-\frac{7}{4}\right) \times \left(-2\frac{3}{8}\right)$

   i. $\frac{3}{4} \cdot \left(-1\frac{5}{6}\right) \cdot \frac{7}{4} \cdot \left(-2\frac{3}{8}\right)$ **j.** $\frac{3}{4} \times 1\frac{5}{6} \times \frac{7}{4} \times \left(-2\frac{3}{8}\right)$

7. You have located fractions such as $-\frac{5}{7}$ on a number line. You have

   also used fractions to show division: $\frac{-5}{7} = -5 \div 7$ and

   $\frac{5}{-7} = 5 \div (-7)$. Tell whether each statement is *true* or *false*. Explain.

   a. $\frac{-1}{2} = \frac{1}{-2}$ **b.** $-\frac{1}{2} = \frac{-1}{-2}$

8. Find a value for n to make each sentence true.

a. $24 \div 2 = n$

b. $-24 \div (-2) = n$

c. $24 \div n = -12$

d. $n \div 2 = -12$

e. $5 \div 2.5 = n$

f. $-12 \div n = 3$

g. $n \div (-3) = -4$

h. $-16 \div \frac{1}{4} = n$

Write four related multiplication and division facts for each set of integers.

Sample $27, 9, 3$

$$9 \times 3 = 27$$
$$3 \times 9 = 27$$
$$27 \div 9 = 3$$
$$27 \div 3 = 9$$

9. $7, -3, -21$

10. $-4, -5, 20$

11. $1.5, -3, -4.5$

Without doing any calculations, determine whether each expression is greater than, less than, or equal to 0.

12. $-1,105.62 \div 24.3$

13. $0 \times (-67)$

14. $-27.5 \times (-63)$

15. $0 \div 89$

16. $-54.9 \div (-3)$

17. $-2,943 \times 1.06$

18. Use the algorithms you developed to find each value. Show your work.

a. $12 \cdot 9$

b. $5 \times (-25)$

c. $-220 \div (-50)$

d. $48 \div (-6)$

e. $-63 \div 9$

f. $\frac{2}{-3} \times \left(-\frac{4}{5}\right)$

g. $\frac{-99}{33}$

h. $-2.7 \div (-0.3)$

i. -36×5

j. $52.5 \div (-7)$

k. $-2\frac{1}{2} \times \left(-\frac{2}{3}\right)$

l. $9 \div 5$

m. $-9 \times (-50)$

n. $-\frac{96}{24}$

o. $6 \times 1\frac{1}{2}$

p. $-\frac{5}{8} \times \frac{8}{5}$

q. $4 \times \left(-1\frac{1}{4}\right)$

r. $-2.5 \times 2\frac{1}{5}$

Go Online
PHSchool.com

For: Multiple-Choice Skills Practice
Web Code: ana-4354

Multiple Choice Find each value.

19. $-24 \div 4$

A. -96

B. -6

C. 6

D. 96

20. $-10 \times (-5)$

F. -50

G. -2

H. 2

J. 50

21. Chris and Elizabeth are making a version of the Integer Product Game in which players need three products in a row to win. What six factors do they need for their game?

Homework Help Online
PHSchool.com
For: Help with Exercise 21
Web Code: ane-4321

Chris and Elizabeth's Product Game

4	−4	6	−6
9	−9	10	−10
15	−15	25	−25

Factors:

Connections

22. Multiply or divide. Show your work.

a. 52×75 **b.** $52 \times (-75)$ **c.** $-2{,}262 \div (-58)$

d. $\frac{2}{3} \times \frac{4}{5}$ **e.** $-9{,}908 \div 89$ **f.** $-7.77 \div (-0.37)$

g. -34×15 **h.** $53.2 \div (-7)$ **i.** $-\frac{2}{3} \times \frac{6}{8}$

j. $90 \div 50$ **k.** $-90 \times (-50)$ **l.** $-108 \div 24$

m. $19.5 \div (-3)$ **n.** -8.4×6 **o.** $6 \times 2\frac{1}{2}$

p. $-3\frac{2}{3} \times (-9)$ **q.** $-4 \times \left(1\frac{1}{4}\right)$ **r.** $-2.5 \times -2\frac{1}{5}$

23. Find integers to make each sentence true.

a. ▨ × ▨ = 30   **b.** ▨ × ▨ = −30   **c.** − 24 ÷ ▨ = ▨

24. On Tuesday, the temperature changes $-2°F$ per hour from noon until 10:00 a.m. the next morning. The temperature at noon on Tuesday is $75°F$.

a. What is the temperature at 4:00 p.m. on Tuesday?

b. What is the temperature at 9:00 a.m. on Wednesday?

c. Plot the (time, temperature) data on a coordinate graph using noon Tuesday as time 0.

d. Describe the pattern of points. How does the pattern relate to the rate of change in temperature?

25. The diagram below shows Mug Wump drawn on a coordinate grid.

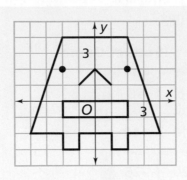

a. Complete the (x, y) column of a table like the one shown to record coordinates of key points needed to draw Mug, or copy your table from Exercise 34 of Investigation 2.

Coordinates for Mug and Variations

Rule	(x, y)	$(2x, 2y)$	$(-2x, -2y)$
Head Outline	$(-4, -2)$		
	$(-2, -2)$		
	$(-2, -3)$		
Nose	$(-1, 1)$		
Mouth	$(-2, -1)$		
Eyes	$(-2, 2)$		

b. Suppose you make scale drawings with rules $(x, y) \rightarrow (2x, 2y)$ and $(x, y) \rightarrow (-2x, -2y)$. Give coordinates for the images of Mug.

c. On graph paper, plot the images of Mug Wump produced by the new sets of coordinates in part (b).

d. Compare the length, width, and area of Mug's mouth to those of the figures drawn in part (c). Explain how you could have predicted those results by studying the coordinate rules for the drawings.

26. Write a number sentence to represent each situation.

   a. The Extraterrestrials have a score of −300. They answer four 50-point questions incorrectly. What is their new score?

   b. The Super Computers answer three 100-point questions incorrectly. They now have 200 points. What was their score before answering the three questions?

   c. The Bigtown Bears football team are at the 25-yard line. In the next three plays, they lose an average of 4 yards per play. Where are the Bears after the three plays?

   d. A new convenience store wants to attract customers. For a one-day special, they sell gasoline for $0.25 below their cost. They sell 5,750 gallons that day. How much money do they lose?

27. The list below gives average temperatures (in °C) for Fairbanks, Alaska, for each month of the year, from January through December.

   −25, −20, −13, −2, 9, 15, 17, 14, 7, −4, −16, −23

   a. What is the median?

   b. What is the range?

   c. What is the mean?

   d. Number the months from 1 (for January) through 12 (for December). Plot a graph of the (month, temperature) data.

28. Find the sum, difference, product, or quotient without using a calculator.

   a. $-5 - 18$

   b. $-23 + 48$

   c. $\frac{3}{4} \times \left(\frac{-5}{9}\right)$

   d. $119 + (-19.3)$

   e. $-1.5 - (-32.8)$

   f. $12 \div 15$

   g. $-169 \div (-1.3)$

   h. $0.47 - 1.56$

   i. $6 \times (-3.5)$

   j. $\frac{2}{-3} \div \frac{5}{6}$

   k. $\frac{7}{12} - \left(-\frac{2}{3}\right)$

   l. $-\frac{4}{5} + \left(-\frac{1}{4}\right)$

29. Estimate the sum, difference, product, or quotient.

a. $-52 - 5$
b. $-43 + (-108)$
c. $2\frac{3}{4} \times \left(-\frac{5}{9}\right)$
d. $79 + (-25.3)$
e. $-12.5 - (-37.3)$
f. $89 \div 15$
g. $-169 \div (-13)$
h. $6.3 - 1.86$
i. $61 \times (-3.9)$
j. $-\frac{2}{3} \div 1\frac{5}{6}$
k. $5\frac{7}{12} - \left(-\frac{2}{3}\right)$
l. $-\frac{4}{5} \div \left(-\frac{1}{4}\right)$

Extensions

30. Many towns and small cities have water towers to store water. Water flows into and out of the towers all day long. Generally, flow out of the tower is greatest during the hours when most people are awake and active. The flow into the tower is greatest at night when most people are asleep.

The table below shows the water flow into and out of a water tower for a given time period. For each part, write a number sentence to find the change in water supply over the given time.

Water Tower Water Flow

	Water Flow In (gallons per hour)	Water Flow Out (gallons per hour)	Time (hours)
a.	5,000	0	4
b.	4,000	0	7
c.	0	7,500	3
d.	5,000	3,000	6.5

31. To add $5 + 3 + 2$, you might think that it is easier to add the $3 + 2$ and then add the answer to the 5. The mathematical property that allows you to change the grouping of addends (or factors) is called the *Associative Property*.

Test the Associative Property for addition and multiplication of integers by simplifying below. Find the values within the parentheses first. When you need a grouping symbol like parentheses inside another parentheses, you can use brackets to make it easier to read. For example, $(4 - (-6))$ can be written as $[4 - (-6)]$.

a. $[3 \times (-3)] \times 4$ and $3 \times (-3 \times 4)$

b. $(-5 \times 4) \times (-3)$ and $-5 \times [4 \times (-3)]$

c. $[-2 \times (-3)] \times (-5)$ and $-2 \times [-3 \times (-5)]$

d. $(3 \times 4) \times (-5)$ and $3 \times [4 \times (-5)]$

e. $[3 + (-3)] + 4$ and $3 + (-3 + 4)$

f. $(-5 + 4) + (-3)$ and $-5 + [4 + (-3)]$

g. $[-2 + (-3)] + (-5)$ and $-2 + [-3 + (-5)]$

h. $(3 + 4) + (-5)$ and $3 + [4 + (-5)]$

i. Does the Associative Property work for addition and multiplication of integers?

32. Explain how each rule changes the original shape, size, and location of Mug Wump.

a. $(x, y) \rightarrow (-x, y)$ **b.** $(x, y) \rightarrow (x, -y)$

c. $(x, y) \rightarrow (-0.5x, -0.5y)$ **d.** $(x, y) \rightarrow (-0.5x, y)$

e. $(x, y) \rightarrow (-3x, -3y)$ **f.** $(x, y) \rightarrow (-3x + 5, -3y - 4)$

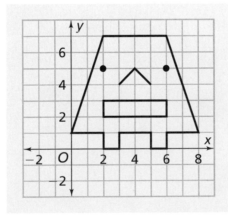

33. Tell whether each statement is *true* or *false*. Explain.

a. $-1 = -1 + 0$ **b.** $-3\frac{3}{8} = -\frac{21}{8}$ **c.** $-6.75 = -6 + \left(-\frac{3}{4}\right)$

34. Find a set of numbers to make a Sum Game. Each sum on the board should be the sum of two numbers (possibly a single number added to itself). Each pair of numbers should add to a sum on the board.

Hint: You need 11 numbers, all with different absolute values.

Sum Game Board

-24	-22	-20	-18	-16	-14
-12	-11	-10	-9	-8	-7
-6	-5	-4	-3	-2	-1
0	1	2	3	4	5
6	7	8	9	10	11
12	14	16	18	20	22

Numbers:

35. Write a story for a problem that is answered by finding the value of *n*.

a. $-4n = -24$ **b.** $\frac{n}{2} = 16$

Mathematical Reflections 3

In the problems of this investigation you studied ways to use multiplication and division of integers to answer questions about speed, time, distance, and direction of motion. You used the results of those calculations to develop algorithms for multiplying and dividing any two integers. The questions that follow should help you to summarize your findings.

Think about your answers to these questions. Discuss your ideas with other students and your teacher. Then write a summary of your findings in your notebook.

1. How do you find the product of two numbers when
   a. both are positive?
   b. one is positive and one is negative?
   c. both are negative?
   d. one is 0?

2. How do you find the quotient of two numbers when
   a. both are positive?
   b. one is positive and the other is negative?
   c. both are negative?
   d. the numerator is 0?

3. Suppose three numbers are related by an equation in the form $a \times b = c$ where a, b, and c are not equal to 0. Write two equivalent number sentences using division.

Properties of Operations

When you learn new types of numbers, you want to know what properties apply to them. You know that rational numbers are commutative for addition and multiplication.

$$-\frac{2}{3} + \frac{1}{6} = \frac{1}{6} + \left(-\frac{2}{3}\right) \text{ and } -\frac{2}{3} \times \frac{1}{6} = \frac{1}{6} \times \left(-\frac{2}{3}\right)$$

In this investigation, you will study another important property of rational numbers. You will also learn a mathematical rule that tells you the order in which to do arithmetic operations.

4.1 Order of Operations

Mathematicians have established rules called the **order of operations** in which to perform operations $(+, -, \times, \div)$. Why do you need such rules?

Rules make this clear:
6 + 20 · 5

The rugby club orders 20 new jerseys. The manufacturer charges a $100 setup fee and $15 per shirt. The total cost is represented by the equation, $C = 100 + 15n$, where C is the cost in dollars and n is the number of jerseys ordered. Pedro and David calculate the amount the club owes.

Pedro's calculation:
$$C = 100 + 15 \times 20$$
$$= 100 + 300$$
$$= \$400$$

David's calculation:
$$C = 100 + 15 \times 20$$
$$= 115 \times 20$$
$$= \$2,300$$

• Who did the calculations correctly?

Order of Operations

1. Compute any expressions within parentheses.

   Example 1

   $(-7 - 2) + 1 =$

   $-9 + 1 = -8$

   Example 2

   $(1 + 2) \times (-4) =$

   $3 \times (-4) = -12$

2. Compute any exponents.

   Example 1

   $-2 + 3^2 =$

   $-2 + 9 = 7$

   Example 2

   $6 - (-1 + 4)^2 =$

   $6 - (3)^2 = -3$

3. Multiply and divide in order from left to right.

   Example 1

   $1 + 2 \times 4 =$ Multiplication first

   $1 + 8 = 9$

   Example 2

   $200 \div 10 \times 2 =$ Division first

   $20 \times 2 = 40$ Multiplication second

4. Add and subtract in order from left to right.

   $1 + 2 - 3 \times 4 =$ Multiplication first

   $1 + 2 - 12 =$ Addition and subtraction

   $3 - 12 = -9$

Use the order of operations in Problem 4.1.

Problem 4.1 Order of Operations

A. In a game, the goal is to write a number sentence that gives the greatest possible result using all the numbers on four cards. Jeremy draws the following four cards.

1. Joshua writes $5 - (-6) \times 4 + (-3) = 41$. Sarah says the result should be 26. Who is correct and why?
2. Wendy starts by writing $-3 \quad (-6) + 5^4 =$. What is her result?
3. Insert parentheses into $-3 - (-6) + 5^4$ to give a greater result than in part (2).

B. Find each value.

1. $-7 \times 4 + 8 \div 2$
2. $(3 + 2)^2 \times 6 - 1$
3. $2\frac{2}{5} \times 4\frac{1}{2} - 5^3 + 3$
4. $8 \times (4 - 5)^3 + 3$
5. $-8 \times [4 - (-5 + 3)]$
6. $-16 \div 8 \times 2^3 + (-7)$

C. Use parentheses, if needed, to make the greatest and least possible values.

1. $7 - 2 + 3^2$
2. $46 + 2.8 \times 7 - 2$
3. $25 \times (-3.12) + 21.3 \div 3$
4. $5.67 + 35.4 - 178 - 181$

D. Use the order of operations to solve this problem. Show your work.

$$3 + 4 \times 5 \div 2 \times 3 - 7^2 + 6 \div 3 = \blacksquare$$

ACE **Homework starts on page 69.**

In this problem, you will compute areas of rectangles using different expressions. Look for ways to rewrite an expression into an equivalent expression that is easier to compute.

Problem 4.2 Distributing Operations

A. Richard lives in a neighborhood with a rectangular field. Each part below shows a way to divide the field for different kinds of sports.

   1. Find the area.

50 yds

120 yds

   2. The field is divided into two parts.

30 yds

20 yds

120 yds

     a. Find the area of each part.

     b. Write a number sentence that shows that the sum of the smaller areas is equal to the area of the entire field.

   3. The field is divided into four parts.

30 yds

20 yds

80 yds   40 yds

     a. Find the area of each part.

     b. Write a number sentence that shows that the sum of the smaller areas is equal to the area of the entire field.

B. Use what you learned in Question A. Write two different expressions to find the area of each rectangle. Tell which uses fewer operations.

1.
2.

3.
4.

C. 1. Draw a rectangle whose area can be represented by $7 \times (11 + 9)$.

   2. Write another expression for the area of the rectangle in part (1).

   3. Draw a rectangle whose area can be represented by $(3 + 1) \times (3 + 4)$.

   4. Write another expression for the area of the rectangle in part (3).

D. The unknown length in each rectangle is represented by a variable x.

   1. Write an expression to represent the area of the rectangle.

   2. Write two different expressions to represent the area of each rectangle below.

   a.
   b.

E. Find the missing part(s) to make each sentence true.

   1. $12 \times (6 + 4) = (12 \times \blacksquare) + (12 \times 4)$

   2. $2 \times (n + 4) = (2 \times \blacksquare) + (\blacksquare \times 4)$

   3. $(n \times 5) + (n \times 3) = \blacksquare \cdot (5 + 3)$

   4 . $(-3 \times 5) + (\blacksquare \times 7) = -3 \cdot (\blacksquare + 7)$

   5. $4n + 11n = n \cdot (\blacksquare + \blacksquare)$

ACE Homework starts on page 69.

4.3 The Distributive Property and Subtraction

The rectangles in Problem 4.2 illustrate an important property of numbers and operations called the **Distributive Property.** This property shows that multiplication *distributes* over addition. When you think about a multiplication problem like 512×5 as $500 \times 5 + 12 \times 5$, or $12 \times 5\frac{3}{4}$ as $12 \times 5 + 12 \times \frac{3}{4}$, you are using the Distributive Property.

Getting Ready for Problem

You can use the Distributive Property to rewrite an expression as one that is easier to calculate or gives new information. You can do this in two ways.

1. Suppose an expression is written as the product of two factors, one of which is a sum. You can use the Distributive Property to multiply one factor by each number in the second factor. This is called *expanding* the expression.

$$-3 \cdot (4 + 8) = -3 \cdot 4 + (-3) \cdot 8$$

With a variable: $-2 \cdot (x + 6) = -2x + (-2) \cdot 6$

2. Suppose an expression is written as a sum and the numbers have a common factor. You can use the Distributive Property to rewrite the expression as the common factor multiplied by the sum. This is called *factoring* the expression.

$$5 \cdot 4 + 5 \cdot 7 = 5 \cdot (4 + 7)$$

With a variable: $8 \cdot 2 + 8x = 8 \cdot (2 + x)$

• Do you think the Distributive Property can be used to expand or factor expressions with subtraction? Explain your reasoning.

A. Use the Distributive Property to expand each expression.

1. $5 \cdot (3 + 2)$ **2.** $5 \cdot [3 + (-2)]$

3. $5 \cdot (3 - 2)$ **4.** $5 \cdot [3 - (-2)]$

5. For parts (1)–(4), find the value of the expression.

6. Does the Distributive Property seem to hold for subtraction? Explain.

B. Use the Distributive Property to expand each expression.

1. $-5 \cdot (3 + 2)$ **2.** $-5 \cdot (3 - 2)$

3. $-5 \cdot [3 + (-2)]$ **4.** $-5 \cdot [3 - (-2)]$

5. For parts (1)–(4), find the value of the expression.

6. Explain how to distribute a negative number to expand an expression.

C. Write each expression in factored form.

1. $6 \cdot 2 + 6 \cdot 3$ **2.** $6 \cdot 2 - 6 \cdot 3$

3. $-6 \cdot 2 + (-6) \cdot 3$ **4.** $-6 \cdot 2 - (-6) \cdot 3$

5. $5x - 8x$ **6.** $-3x - 4x$

7. Explain how to factor an expression with subtraction.

D. Three friends are going hiking. Lisa buys 2 bottles of water and 3 packs of trail mix for each of them.

1. Can she go through the express checkout lane for customers with 15 or fewer items?

2. Write a number sentence to show how you found the total number of items.

3. Write another number sentence to find the total number of items.

E. Mr. Chan bought a roll of kitchen towels for $1.19 and window cleaner for $2.69. In his state there is a 4% sales tax on these items.

1. What is his total bill?

2. Write a number sentence to show how you found the total bill.

3. Suppose you add the prices of the two items and then compute the tax. Your friend finds the tax on each item and then adds the two together. Which method is better? Explain.

ACE Homework starts on page 69.

More on Notation

Now you can use the order of operations or the Distributive Property to find the value of an expression like $-8 \cdot [-2 + (-3)]$ that has parentheses.

Order of operations method:

$$-8 \cdot [-2 + (-3)] = -8 \cdot (-5) \qquad \text{Add } -2 \text{ and } -3 \text{ within the parentheses.}$$

$$= 40 \qquad \text{Multiply.}$$

Distributive Property method:

$$-8 \cdot [-2 + (-3)] = -8 \cdot (-2) + (-8) \cdot (-3) \qquad \text{Expand first.}$$

$$= 16 + 24 \qquad \text{Multiply.}$$

$$= 40$$

Either method is correct.

Applications

1. Find the values of each pair of expressions.

    a. $-12 + (-4 + 9)$ $[-12 + (-4)] + 9$

    b. $(14 - 20) - 2^3$ $14 - (20 - 2^3)$

    c. $[14 + (-20)] + -8$ $14 + [-20 + (-8)]$

    d. $-1 - [-1 + (-1)]$ $[-1 - (-1)] + (-1)$

    e. Which cases lead to expressions with different results? Explain.

2. Find the value of each expression.

    a. $(5 - 3) \div (-2) \times (-1)$ **b.** $2 + (-3) \times 4 - (-5)$

    c. $4 \times 2 \times (-3) + (-10) \div 5$ **d.** $-3 \times [2 + (-10)] - 2^2$

    e. $(4 - 20) \div 2^2 - 5 \times (-2)$ **f.** $10 - [50 \div (-2 \times 25) - 7] \times 2^2$

3. Draw and label the edges and areas of a rectangle to illustrate each pair of equivalent expressions.

    a. $(3 + 2) \cdot 12 = 3 \cdot 12 + 2 \cdot 12$

    b. $9 \cdot 3 + 9 \cdot 5 = 9 \cdot (3 + 5)$

    c. $x \cdot (5 + 9) = 5x + 9x$

    d. $2 \cdot (x + 8) = 2x + 16$

Homework Help Online
PHSchool.com
For: Help with Exercise 3
Web Code: ane-4403

4. Write equivalent expressions to show two different ways to find the area of each rectangle. Use the ideas of the Distributive Property.

a.

b.

c.

d.

5. Rewrite each expression in an equivalent form to show a simpler way to do the arithmetic. Explain how you know the two results are equal without doing any calculations.

    a. $(-150 + 270) + 30$

    b. $(43 \times 120) + [43 \times (-20)]$

    c. $23 + (-75) + 14 + (-23) - (-75)$

    d. $(0.8 \times -23) + (0.8 \times -7)$

6. Without doing any calculations, determine whether each number sentence is true. Explain. Then check your answer.

    a. $50 \times 432 = (50 \times 400) + (50 \times 32)$

    b. $50 \times 368 = (50 \times 400) - (50 \times 32)$

    c. $-50 \times (-800) = (-50 \times (-1{,}000)) + (-50 \times 200)$

    d. $-50 + (400 \times 32) = (-50 + 400) \times (-50 + 32)$

    e. $(-70 \times 20) + (-50 \times 20) = (-120) \times 20$

    f. $6 \times 17 = 6 \times 20 - 6 \times 3$

7. For each part, use the Distributive Property to write an equivalent expression.

    a. $-2 \times [5 + (-8)]$ **b.** $(-3 \cdot 2) - [-3 \cdot (-12)]$

    c. $x \cdot (-3 + 5)$ **d.** $(-7x) + (4x)$

    e. $2x \cdot [2 - (-4)]$ **f.** $(x) - (3x)$

Connections

Find the sum, difference, product, or quotient.

8. $-10 \times (-11)$ **9.** -10×11

10. $10 - 11$ **11.** $-3 \div (-12)$

12. $3^2 \times 2^2$ **13.** $3^2 \times (-2)^2$

14. $-24 - (-12)$ **15.** $\dfrac{-24}{-12}$

16. $-48 \div 4^2$ **17.** 50×70

18. $50 \times (-70)$ **19.** $2{,}200 \div (-22)$

20. $-50 \times (-120)$ **21.** $-139 + 899$

22. $5{,}600 - 7{,}800$ **23.** $-4{,}400 - (-1{,}200)$

24. $\dfrac{-9{,}900}{-99}$ **25.** $-580 + (-320)$

For: Multiple-Choice Skills Practice

Web Code: ana-4454

26. When using negative numbers and exponents, parentheses are sometimes needed to make it clear what you are multiplying.

-5^4 can be thought of as "the opposite of 5^4" or
$-(5^4) = -(5 \cdot 5 \cdot 5 \cdot 5) = -625$

$(-5)^4$ can be thought of as "negative five to the fourth power" or
$-5 \cdot (-5) \cdot (-5) \cdot (-5) = 625$

Indicate whether each expression will be negative or positive.

a. -3^2 **b.** $(-6)^3$ **c.** $(-4)^4$ **d.** -1^6 **e.** $(-3)^4$

27. The following list shows the yards gained and lost on each play by the Mathville Mudhens in the fourth quarter of their last football game:

$$-8, 20, 3, 7, -15, 4, -12, 32, 5, 1$$

Write an expression that shows how to compute their average gain or loss per play. Then compute the average.

28. Complete each number sentence.

a. $-34 + (-15) = \blacksquare$ **b.** $-12 \times (-23) = \blacksquare$

c. $-532 \div (-7) = \blacksquare$ **d.** $-777 - (-37) = \blacksquare$

e. Write a fact family for part (a).   **f.** Write a fact family for part (b).

29. Write a related fact. Use it to find the value of n that makes the sentence true.

a. $n - (-5) = 35$ **b.** $4 + n = -43$

c. $-2n = -16$ **d.** $\frac{n}{4} = -32$

30. Multiple Choice Which set of numbers is in order from least to greatest?

    A. 31.4,   −14.2,   −55, 75,   −0.05,   0.5,   3.140

    B. $\dfrac{2}{5}$, $\dfrac{-3}{5}$, $\dfrac{8}{7}$, $\dfrac{-9}{8}$, $\dfrac{-3}{2}$, $\dfrac{5}{3}$

    C. −0.2,   −0.5,   0.75,   0.6,   −1,   1.5

    D. None of these

31. Find the absolute values of the numbers for each set in Exercise 30. Write them in order from least to greatest.

32. A trucking company carries freight along a highway from New York City to San Francisco. Its home base is in Omaha, Nebraska, which is about halfway between the two cities. Truckers average about 50 miles per hour on this route.

Make a number line to represent this truck route. Put Omaha at 0. Use positive numbers for cities east of Omaha and negative numbers for cities west of Omaha. Then write number sentences to answer each question.

    a. A truck leaves Omaha heading east and travels for 7 hours. About how far does the truck go? Where on the number line does it stop?

b. A truck leaves Omaha heading west and travels for 4.5 hours. About how far does the truck go? Where on the number line does it stop?

c. A truck heading east arrives in Omaha. About where on the number line was the truck 12 hours earlier?

d. A truck heading west arrives in Omaha. About where on the number line was the truck 11 hours earlier?

33. Insert parentheses (or brackets) in each expression where needed to show how to get each result.

    a. $1 + (-3) \times (-4) = 8$ **b.** $1 + (-3) \times (-4) = 13$

    c. $-6 \div (-2) + (-4) = 1$ **d.** $-6 \div (-2) + (-4) = -1$

    e. $-4 \times 2 - 10 = -18$ **f.** $-4 \times 2 - 10 = 32$

34. A grocery store receipt shows 5% state tax due on laundry detergent and a flower bouquet.

Laundry Detergent	$7.99	T
Flower Bouquet	$3.99	T

Does it matter whether the tax is calculated on each separate item or the total cost? Explain.

35. You can use dot patterns to illustrate distributive properties for operations on whole numbers. Write a number sentence to represent the pair of dot patterns.

 =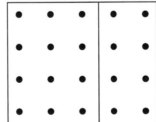

Extensions

Copy each pair of expressions in Exercises 36–40. Insert < or > to make a true statement.

36. -23 ■ -45

37. $-23 + 10$ ■ $-45 + 10$

38. $-23 - 10$ ■ $-45 - 10$

39. -23×10 ■ -45×10

40. $-23 \times (-10)$ ■ $-45 \times (-10)$

Based on your results in Exercises 36–40, complete each statement. Test your ideas with other numerical cases, or develop another kind of explanation, perhaps using chip board or number line ideas.

41. If $a > b$, then $a + c$ ■ $b + c$.

42. If $a > b$, then $a - c$ ■ $b - c$.

43. If $a > b$, then $a \times c$ ■ $b \times c$.

44. Find the value for n that makes the sentence true.

    a. $n - (-24) = 12$ **b.** $2.5n = -10$ **c.** $2.5n + (-3) = -13$

45. Complete each pair of calculations.

    a. $12 \div (-8 + 4) =$ ■ $[12 \div (-8)] + (12 \div 4) =$ ■

    b. $-12 \div [-5 - (-3)] =$ ■ $[-12 \div (-5)] - [-12 \div (-3)] =$ ■

    c. $4 \div (-2 - 6) =$ ■ $(4 \div -2) - (4 \div 6) =$ ■

    d. $3 \div (5 + 6) =$ ■ $(3 \div 5) + (3 \div 6) =$ ■

    e. What can you conclude from parts (a)–(d) about the Distributive Property?

46. When you find the mean (average) of two numbers, you add them together and divide by 2.

    a. Is the operation of finding the average of two numbers commutative? Give examples.

    b. Does multiplication distribute over the averaging operation? That is, will a number a times the average of two numbers, x and y, give the same thing as the average of ax and ay? Give examples.

Mathematical Reflections 4

In this investigation, you compared important properties of arithmetic with positive numbers to properties of arithmetic with negative numbers. The following questions will help you summarize what you have learned.

Think about your answers. Discuss your ideas with other students and your teacher. Then write a summary of your findings in your notebook.

1. **a.** What is the order of operations? Why is it important for you to understand?

   b. Give an example of an equation where the use of parentheses changes the result of the computation.

2. **a.** What does it mean to say that an operation is *commutative?*

   b. Which operations on integers are commutative? Give numerical examples.

3. What does it mean to say that *multiplication distributes over addition* and *subtraction*? Give numerical examples.

Unit Project

Dealing Down

Dealing Down is a mathematics card game that tests your creative skill at writing expressions. Play several rounds of the game. Then write a report on the strategies you found.

How to Play Dealing Down

- Work in small groups.
- Shuffle the 25 cards marked with the following numbers.
$-10, -9, -8, -7, -6, -5, -4, -3, -2, -1, -\frac{1}{2}, -\frac{1}{3}, -\frac{1}{4}, 0,$
$0.25, \frac{1}{3}, 0.5, 1, 2, 3, 4, 5, 7, 8, 10$
- Deal four cards to the center of the table.
- All players use the four numbers to write an expression with the least possible quantity.
- Players compare answers and discuss how they know their quantity is accurate and the least possible.
- Each player with an expression for the least quantity gets 1 point.
- Record the results of that round in a table like the one below and play more rounds.

Round 1

Cards Dealt	Expression With the Least Quantity	Who Scored a Point
Why That Expression Has the Least Quantity:		

- The player with the most points at the end of the game wins.

Write a Report

Write a report about strategies for writing the least possible quantity using four numbers.

Consider the following ideas as you look at the strategies in Dealing Down.

- Operating with negative and positive numbers
- Order of operations including the use of parentheses and exponents
- Commutative Property of Addition and Multiplication
- Distributive Property

Looking Back and Looking Ahead

Unit Review

In this unit, you investigated properties, operations, and applications of integers. You learned how to

Go Online
PHSchool.com

For: Vocabulary Review Puzzle
Web Code: anj-4051

- Add, subtract, multiply and divide with integers
- Represent integers and operations on a chip board and a number line
- Use integers in real-world problems

Use Your Understanding: Integers and Rational Numbers

Test your understanding of integers by solving the following problems.

1. An absent-minded scorekeeper writes the number sentences below. Find the value of n that makes each sentence true. Explain what each sentence tells about the rounds of play.

   a. BrainyActs: $-250 + (-100) + 200 + n = 50$

   b. MathXperts: $450 + (-250) + n = 0$

   c. ExCells: $n + 50 + 200 + (-150) = -250$

   d. SuperM's: $350 + (-300) + n = -150$

2. Irving goes to college 127 miles away from home. When he drives home for vacation, he plans to drop off his friend, Whitney, along the way. Her exit is 93 miles before his exit,

   Irving and Whitney are so busy talking that they miss the exit to her house. They are now only 36 miles from Irving's exit! How far do they have to travel in all from college until they finally reach Whitney's exit? Model this problem on a number line.

3. **a.** Write a fact family for each sentence.

   i. $-2\frac{1}{2} + n = -3\frac{3}{4}$ **ii.** $\frac{2}{3}n = 10$

   b. Which member of each fact family would make it easy to solve for n? Explain.

   c. Find the value for n that makes each sentence true.

4. a. Locate point $(5, 2)$ on a coordinate grid.

  b. Find a related point in each quadrant by changing the sign of one or both coordinates.

  i. Quadrant II   **ii.** Quadrant III   **iii.** Quadrant IV

  c. Connect these points in order. Describe the figure formed.

  d. Make a similar figure with an area four times as large and that has a vertex in each quadrant. Give the four vertices as ordered pairs.

Explain Your Reasoning

Answer the following questions to summarize what you know now.

5. Describe what a number line looks like now that the number system has been extended to include negative numbers.

6. Which number is greater? Explain.

  a. $-20, -35$ **b.** $-2\frac{3}{4}, -2\frac{1}{3}$ **c.** $-12.5, 10.5$

7. Use a number line or chip model to check each calculation. Show your work.

  a. $5 + (-7) = -2$ **b.** $-2 + (-9) = -11$

  c. $3 \times (-2) = -6$ **d.** $-3 \times (-2) = 6$

  e. Describe how a number line and chip model can be used to model an addition or multiplication problem.

8. Suppose you are given two integers. How do you find their

  a. sum?   **b.** difference?

  c. product?   **d.** quotient?

9. Which operations with integers have the following properties? Give numerical examples.

  a. commutative   **b.** distributive

Look Ahead

Positive and negative numbers are useful in solving a variety of problems that involve losses and gains. They also provide coordinates for points on an extended number line and coordinate plane. These ideas will be useful when you study graphs of functions and solve equations in future *Connected Mathematics* units such as *Moving Straight Ahead*, *Thinking With Mathematical Models*, *Say It With Symbols*, and *The Shapes of Algebra*.

English/Spanish Glossary

A

absolute value The absolute value of a number is its distance from 0 on a number line. It can be thought of as the value of a number when its sign is ignored. For example, −3 and 3 both have an absolute value of 3.

valor absoluto El valor absoluto de un número es su distancia de 0 sobre una recta numérica. Se puede interpretar como el valor de un número cuando no importa su signo. Por ejemplo, tanto −3 como 3 tienen un valor absoluto de 3.

algorithm A set of rules for performing a procedure. Mathematicians invent algorithms that are useful in many kinds of situations. Some examples of algorithms are the rules for long division or the rules for adding two fractions.

algoritmo Un conjunto de reglas para realizar un procedimiento. Los matemáticos inventan algoritmos que son útiles en muchos tipos de situaciones. Algunos ejemplos de algoritmos son las reglas para una división larga o las reglas para sumar dos fracciones.

Associative Property Allows addends or factors to be grouped and computed in different arrangements. For example, 2 + 3 + 5 can be grouped as (2 + 3) + 5 or 2 + (3 + 5). So, (2 + 3) + 5 = 5 + 5 = 10 and 2 + (3 + 5) = 2 + 8 = 10. This property does not work for subtraction or division. For example, 8 − (4 − 2) ≠ (8 − 4) − 2 and 8 ÷ (4 ÷ 2) ≠ (8 ÷ 4) ÷ 2.

propiedad asociativa Permite que sumandos o factores se agrupen y se calculen de diferentes maneras. Por ejemplo, 2 + 3 + 5 se puede agrupar como (2 + 3) + 5 ó 2 + (3 + 5). Por lo tanto, (2 + 3) + 5 = 5 + 5 = 10 y 2 + (3 + 5) = 2 + 8 = 10. Esta propiedad no funciona con la resta o la división. Por ejemplo, 8 − (4 − 2) ≠ (8 − 4) − 2 y 8 ÷ (4 ÷ 2) ≠ (8 ÷ 4) ÷ 2.

C

Commutative Property The order of the addition or multiplication of two numbers does not change the result. For two numbers a and b, $a + b = b + a$, and $a \cdot b = b \cdot a$.

propiedad conmutativa El orden en la suma o multiplicación de dos números no afecta el resultado. Para dos números a y b, $a + b = b + a$, y $a \cdot b = b \cdot a$.

D

Distributive Property The Distributive Property shows how multiplication combines with addition or subtraction. For three numbers a, b, and c, $a(b + c) = ab + ac$.

propiedad distributiva La propiedad distributiva muestra cómo la multiplicación se combina con la suma o la resta. Para tres números a, b y c, $a(b + c) = ab + ac$.

I

integers The whole numbers and their opposites. 0 is an integer, but is neither positive nor negative. The integers from −4 to 4 are shown on the number line below.

enteros Números enteros positivos y sus opuestos. 0 es un entero, pero no es ni positivo ni negativo. En la siguiente recta numérica figuran los enteros comprendidos entre −4 y 4.

$$-4 \quad -3 \quad -2 \quad -1 \quad 0 \quad 1 \quad 2 \quad 3 \quad 4$$

inverse operations Operations that "undo" each other. Addition and subtraction are inverse operations. For example, start with 7. Subtract 4. Then add 4. You are back to the original number 7. Thus, $7 - 4 + 4 = 7$. Multiplication and division are inverse operations. For example, start with 12. Multiply by 2. Then divide by 2. You are back at the original number 12. Thus, $(12 \times 2) \div 2 = 12$.

operaciones inversas Operaciones que se "anulan" mutuamente. La suma y la resta son operaciones inversas. Por ejemplo, empieza con 7. Resta 4. Luego, suma 4. Tienes otra vez el número 7. Por eso, $7 - 4 + 4 = 7$. La multiplicación y la división son operaciones inversas. Por ejemplo, empieza con 12. Multiplica por 2. Luego, divide por 2. Tienes otra vez el número 12. Por eso, $(12 \times 2) \div 2 = 12$.

N

negative number A number less than 0. On a number line, negative numbers are located to the left of 0 (on a vertical number line, negative numbers are located below 0).

número negativo Un número menor que 0. En una recta numérica, los números negativos están ubicados a la izquierda del 0 (en una recta numérica vertical, los números negativos están ubicados debajo del 0).

number sentence A mathematical statement that gives the relationship between two expressions that are composed of numbers and operation signs. For example, $3 + 2 = 5$ and $6 \times 2 > 10$ are number sentences; $3 + 2, 5, 6 \times 2$, and 10 are expressions.

oración numérica Un enunciado matemático que describe la relación entre dos expresiones compuestas por números y signos de operaciones. Por ejemplo, $3 + 2 = 5$ y $6 \times 2 > 10$ son oraciones numéricas. $3 + 2, 5, 6 \times 2$ y 10 son expresiones.

O

opposites Two numbers whose sum is 0. For example, -3 and 3 are opposites. On a number line, opposites are the same distance from 0 but in different directions from 0. The number 0 is its own opposite.

opuestos Dos números cuya suma da 0. Por ejemplo, -3 y 3 son opuestos. En una recta numérica, los opuestos se encuentran a la misma distancia de 0 pero en distintos sentidos. El número 0 es su propio opuesto.

order of operations Established order in which to perform mathematical operations.
1. Compute any expressions within parentheses.
2. Compute any exponents.
3. Multiply and divide in order from left to right.
4. Add and subtract in order from left to right.

orden de operaciones Orden establecido en el cual se deben realizar las operaciones matemáticas.
1. Calcular cualquier expresión dentro del paréntesis.
2. Calcular cualquier exponente.
3. Multiplicar y dividir de izquierda a derecha.
4. Sumar y restar de izquierda a derecha.

P

positive number A number greater than 0. (The number 0 is neither positive nor negative.) On a number line, positive numbers are located to the right of 0 (on a vertical number line, positive numbers are located above 0).

número positivo Un número mayor que 0. (El número 0 no es ni positivo ni negativo.) En una recta numérica, los números positivos se ubican a la derecha del 0 (en una recta numérica vertical, los números positivos están por encima del 0).

English/Spanish Glossary

quadrants The four sections into which the coordinate plane is divided by the *x*- and *y*-axes. The quadrants are labeled as follows:

cuadrantes Las cuatro secciones en las que un plano de coordenadas queda dividido por los ejes *x* e *y*. Los cuadrantes se identifican de la siguiente manera:

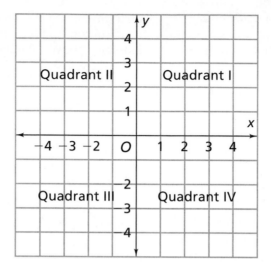

rational numbers Numbers that can be expressed as a quotient of two integers where the divisor is not zero. For example, $\frac{1}{2}, \frac{9}{11}$, and $-\frac{7}{5}$ are rational numbers. Also, 0.799 is a rational number, since $0.799 = \frac{799}{1,000}$.

números racionales Números que se pueden expresar como un cociente de dos números enteros donde el divisor no es cero. Por ejemplo, $\frac{1}{2}, \frac{9}{11}$ y $-\frac{7}{5}$ son números racionales. También 0.799 es un número racional, porque $0.799 = \frac{799}{1,000}$.

Index

Absolute value, 26, 35, 39, 58, 72, 80
   definition, 26, 80

Addition, 22–24, 28–30, 41, 60–68, 75, 78–79
   ACE, 32–40, 55–58, 69–71, 73–74
   algorithm for, 23–24, 32, 41
   Associative Property of, 57
   Commutative Property of, 24, 77, 80
   integer, 22–24, 41
   inverse of subtraction, 28–30

Algorithm
   definition, 22, 80
   for addition, 23–24, 32, 41
   for division, 47–48, 52
   for multiplication, 45–46, 52
   for subtraction, 27, 33, 41

Area model, 64–65, 69
   making, 65, 69

Associative Property, 57, 80
   for addition and multiplication, 57
   for subtraction and division, 80

Check for reasonableness, 24, 27, 70

Chip board, 14–15, 23–25, 28, 34, 79
   ACE, 18, 33, 40
   integer addition and subtraction on, 14–15, 23–25, 28, 33, 34, 79
   integer multiplication on, 40, 79
   using, 15, 18, 24, 33–34, 79

Commutative operations, 24, 27, 45, 48, 60, 74, 75, 77, 79, 80

Commutative Property, 24, 27, 77, 80
   of addition, 24, 77, 80
   definition, 24, 80
   of multiplication, 77, 80
   and subtraction, 27

Comparison, 11–13, 21, 27, 79
   ACE, 16–20, 34–36, 39, 51–52, 54–55, 57–58, 70, 72, 74
   integer, 11

Coordinate graph, 30–31, 82
   ACE, 36–39, 54, 57
   making, 31, 36–38, 54

Coordinate grid, *see* **Coordinate graph**

Coordinate rule, 38, 54, 57
   writing, 38

Dealing Down, 76–77

Diagram, 6

Distributive operations, 64–68, 75, 77, 79, 80
   ACE, 69–71, 73–74

Distributive Property, 66–68, 77, 80
   ACE, 69–70, 73–74
   subtraction and, 66–67, 80

Division, 62–63, 78
   ACE, 50–58, 69–71, 73–74
   algorithm for, 47–48, 52
   Associative Property and, 80
   integer, 47–48, 59
   inverse of multiplication, 47

Dot pattern, 51, 73

Fact family, 30, 36, 47, 52, 71, 78

Game
   Dealing Down, 76–77
   Integer Product Game, 48–49, 53
   MathMania, 8–9, 16, 38, 55, 78
   Sum Game, 58

Golf, positive and negative scores in, 12

Graph
   coordinate, *see* Coordinate graph
   making, 55

Integer
   ACE, 16–20, 32–40, 50–58, 69–74
   addition, 22–24, 41
   comparison, 11
   definition, 6, 80
   division, 47–48, 59
   multiplication, 44–46, 49, 59
   opposites, 6, 81
   order, 11

   patterns, 29, 46–47
   subtraction, 24–27

Integer Product Game, 48–49, 53

Interpreting data
   area model, 64–65, 69
   chip board, 14–15, 18, 23–25, 28, 33–34, 40, 79
   coordinate graph, 30–31, 36–39, 54, 57, 82
   dot pattern, 51, 73
   diagram, 6
   graph, 55
   number line, 5–7, 10–13, 16–18, 21, 23–24, 26–27, 32, 35, 40, 44, 50–51, 72–73, 78–79, 80
   picture, 10, 26, 28, 34, 63, 72
   table, 8–9, 15, 16, 18–20, 24, 27, 34, 40, 45, 47–49, 53–54, 56, 58, 76
   thermometer, 10, 13

Inverse operations
   addition and subtraction, 28–30
   definition, 81
   multiplication and division, 47

Investigations
   Adding and Subtracting Integers, 22–41
   Extending the Number System, 5–21
   Multiplying and Dividing Integers, 42–59
   Properties of Operations, 60–75

Justify answer, 45–46, 48, 66–67, 78
   ACE, 34, 36, 39–40, 51, 54, 58, 69–70, 73

Justify method, 67

Looking Back and Looking Ahead: Unit Reflections, 78–79

Manipulatives
   Integer Product Game, 48–49
   chip board, 15, 18, 24, 33–34, 79

Mathematical Highlights, 4

Mathematical Reflections, 21, 41, 59, 75

MathMania, 8–9, 16, 38, 55, 78

Model
    area model, 64–65, 69
    chip board, 14–15, 18, 23, 25, 28, 33, 40
    dot pattern, 51, 73
    number line, 5–6, 10–13, 17–18, 23, 26, 32, 35, 40, 44, 50, 72, 80
    picture, 10, 26, 28, 34, 63, 72
    thermometer, 10

Multiplication, 44–46, 49, 59, 60–68, 75, 78–79
    ACE, 50–58, 69–74
    algorithm for, 45–46, 52
    Associative Property of, 57
    Commutative Property of, 77, 80
    Distributive Property and, 66–68, 69–70, 73–74, 77, 80
    integer, 44–46, 49, 59
    Integer Product Game, 48–49, 53
    inverse of division, 47

Negative number
    definition, 3, 5, 81
    exponents and, 71
    notation for, 5, 7, 42

Notation, 5–7, 13, 27, 42, 68, 71
    brackets, *see* parentheses
    minus, 5, 7, 42
    for negative numbers, 5, 7, 42
    operation, 7, 42
    opposites, 42
    parentheses, 42, 68, 71
    plus, 6, 7, 42
    for positive numbers, 6, 7, 42

Notebook, 21, 41, 59, 75

Number
    integer, 6, 80
    negative, 3, 5, 81
    opposites, 6, 81
    positive, 3, 6, 81
    rational, 6, 82

Number line, 5–7, 10–13, 21, 23–24, 26–27, 44, 78–79, 80
    absolute value on, 26

ACE, 16–18, 32, 35, 40, 50–51, 72–73
    adding integers on, 23–24, 26, 32, 40, 78–79
    locating integers on, 10–13, 16–18, 21, 51
    making, 5, 11, 13, 16–17, 24, 39, 72–73, 78–79
    multiplying integers on, 44, 50, 72–73, 79
    subtracting integers on, 23, 26–27, 78–79
    thermometer as, 10

Number sentence, definition, 81

Operations
    commutative, 24, 27, 45, 48, 60, 74, 75, 77, 79, 80
    distributive, 64–68, 69–71, 73–74, 75, 77, 79, 80
    order of, 60–63, 68, 75, 77, 81

Opposites
    definition, 6, 81
    integer, 6–7, 11, 31, 37, 42, 71, 81
    notation for, 42

Order, 11
    ACE, 16, 19, 38, 72
    integer, 11

Order of operations, 60–63, 68, 75, 77, 81

Pattern
    integer addition and subtraction, 29
    integer division, 47
    integer multiplication, 46
    looking for, 29, 46–47, 53, 73

Picture, 10, 26, 28, 34, 63, 72

Positive number
    definition, 3, 6, 81
    notation for, 6, 7, 42

Problem-solving strategies
    looking for a pattern, 29, 46–47, 53, 73
    making an area model, 65, 69

making a coordinate graph, 31, 36–38, 54
    making a graph, 55
    making a number line, 5, 11, 13, 16–17, 24, 39, 72–73, 78–79
    making a table, 15, 18, 20, 54, 58, 76
    solving an easier problem, 64–65, 70
    using an algorithm, 23–24, 27, 32–33, 41, 45–48, 52
    using a chip board, 15, 18, 24, 33–34, 79
    using a thermometer, 10, 13
    writing a coordinate rule, 38

Quadrant, 31, 79, 82

Rational number, definition, 6, 82

Reasonableness, *see* **Check for reasonableness**

Solving an easier problem, 64–65, 70

Subtraction, 62–63, 67, 75
    ACE, 32–40, 55–56, 69–71, 73–74
    algorithm for, 27, 33, 41
    Associative Property and, 80
    Commutative Property and, 27
    Distributive Property and, 66–67, 80
    integer, 24–27
    inverse of addition, 28–30

Sum Game, 58

Table, 8–9, 15, 24, 27, 45, 47–49, 76
    ACE, 16, 18–20, 34, 40, 53–54, 56, 58
    making, 15, 18, 20, 54, 58, 76

Temperature
    ACE, 17, 20, 34, 38, 53, 55
    integers and, 10–13, 23

Thermometer
    as a number line, 10
    using, 10, 13

Unit Project, 76–77

Acknowledgments

Team Credits

The people who made up the **Connected Mathematics 2** team—representing editorial, editorial services, design services, and production services—are listed below. Bold type denotes core team members.

Leora Adler, Judith Buice, Kerry Cashman, Patrick Culleton, Sheila DeFazio, Katie Hallahan, Richard Heater, **Barbara Hollingdale, Jayne Holman,** Karen Holtzman, **Etta Jacobs,** Christine Lee, Carolyn Lock, Catherine Maglio, **Dotti Marshall,** Rich McMahon, Eve Melnechuk, Kristin Mingrone, Terri Mitchell, **Marsha Novak,** Irene Rubin, Donna Russo, Robin Samper, Siri Schwartzman, **Nancy Smith,** Emily Soltanoff, **Mark Tricca,** Paula Vergith, Roberta Warshaw, Helen Young

Additional Credits

Diana Bonfilio, Mairead Reddin, Michael Torocsik, nSight, Inc.

Technical Illustration

WestWords, Inc.

Cover Design

tom white.images

Photos

2, Richard Haynes; **3,** AP Photo/Jonathan Hayward; **5,** Richard Haynes; **8,** Richard Haynes; **10,** Stephanie Maze/Corbis; **12,** AP Photo/Gregory Smith; **14,** PhotoDisc/Getty Images, Inc.; **17,** Josh Mitchell/Getty Images, Inc.; **22,** Creatas/AGE Fotostock; **28,** Richard Haynes; **37,** Creatas/PictureQuest; **43,** Paul J. Sutton/Corbis; **50,** Dennis MacDonald/PhotoEdit; **53,** Spencer Grant/PhotoEdit; **56,** SuperStock, Inc./SuperStock; **60,** Richard Haynes; **61,** Syracuse Newspapers/The Image Works; **64,** Tom Carter/PhotoEdit; **71,** Dennis MacDonald/Index Stock Imagery, Inc.; **77,** Richard Haynes